THE CROCHETER'S GUIDE TO

Yarn Cocktails

QUARRY

THE CROCHETER'S GUIDE TO

Yarn Cocktails

30 Technique-Expanding Recipes for Tasty Little Projects

GLOUCESTER MASSACHUSETTS

QUARRY BOOKS

Anastasia Blaes and Kelly Wilson

First published in the United States of America by
Quarry Books, a member of
Quayside Publishing Group
33 Commercial Street
Gloucester, Massachusetts 01930-5089
Telephone: (978) 282-9590
Fax: (978) 283-2742
www.quarrybooks.com

Library of Congress Cataloging-in-Publication Data
Blaes, Anastasia.
   The crocheter's guide to yarn cocktails : 30 technique-expanding recipes for tasty little projects / by Anastasia Blaes and Kelly Wilson.
        p.   cm.
     ISBN-13: 978-1-59253-318-3
     ISBN-10: 1-59253-318-3
     1. Crocheting—Patterns. I. Wilson, Kelly. II. Title.
   TT825.B544 2007
   746.43'4041—dc22   2006031348
                                                        CIP

ISBN-13: 978-1-59253-318-3
ISBN-10: 1-59253-318-3

10 9 8 7 6 5 4 3 2 1

Design: Judy Morgan
Photography: Allan Penn, except for pages 29, 31, 54, 85, 88, and 123 by Glenn Scott Photography
Illustrations: Judy Love
Technical Editing and Schematics: Jean Lampe

Printed in China

Yarns shown on cover (left to right): Blue Heron Yarns Rayon Softwist in Kelp, Tilli Tomas Mariel's Crystals in Natural, Blue Sky Alpacas Alpaca and Silk in #136, Kolláge Yarns Serenity in Sandy Beach, and Alpaca with a Twist Big Baby in Autumn Leaves. Swarovski crystals and Kolláge Yarns Accentables are sprinkled in front of the cocktails.

To Mom and Katie—A. B.

To Jim and Zack—K.W.

Menu

Introduction

Welcome to the *Yarn Cocktails* Lounge!

Looking for some cool refreshment? Unwind after a long, hard day with a *Yarn Cocktails* pattern! Inspired by popular drinks, *Yarn Cocktails* designs are relaxing crochet patterns that explore new techniques in tasty sips. Each pattern focuses on a specific technique, so you can slow down and fully master a new skill while savoring the sensuous process of using luscious yarns to create a unique, touchable cocktail.

The Crocheter's Guide to Yarn Cocktails is meant to be used as a reference as well as a compilation of exciting patterns. To guide you, the *Yarn Cocktails* menu (see previous page) is divided according to drink category and crochet technique. Experienced crocheters can browse the menu to select a project for their crochet refreshment; crocheters who wish to expand their skills will find a detailed explanation of each technique at the beginning of each chapter. Projects become more challenging as the chapter goes on, introducing new applications of each technique. In turn, each chapter builds on the skills learned in the previous one. This step-by-step approach will prepare even beginning crocheters for intricate projects. By the time you have completed all the projects, you will be an accomplished crocheter with a wardrobe full of your own handmade, luxurious creations!

As you read through the chapters, symbols will guide you. Not sure if you've learned the techniques needed to complete the project? Look for the Refresh ice cube at the top of the pattern, which will list the techniques needed to successfully complete the project and where they are located in the book. Olives at the top of the pattern indicate its difficulty level: the more olives, the more challenging the project. For designer tips that will give your creation a professional finish, check out the martini glasses.

Yarn Cocktails designs are relaxing, instructive, and portable— perfect for busy lifestyles. They offer something for everyone, from a vest and a necktie for the men to necklaces and skirts for the ladies. So, have a seat, kick off your shoes, and quench your thirst for crocheted refreshment!

& Kelly

www.anastasiaknits.com

Ingredients

Tools of the Trade

Hooks

With the exception of steel, all of the following hooks are sized with letters and numbers; the higher the number, the fatter the hook.

Aluminum—These hooks can be slippery. You can crochet even faster by rubbing them with hand lotion or waxed paper.

Bamboo and Wood—Warm to the hand, hooks made of these materials are lightweight; great for crocheting with lightweight, slippery fibers.

Plastic or Acrylic—Light-color hooks work well with darker yarns. A translucent hook works well with eyelash and other novelties.

Steel—Hooks of steel are great for poking through fabrics to create edgings and for working with thread. They are sized by numbers; the higher the number, the smaller the diameter of the hook.

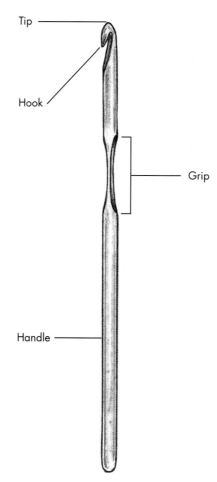

Anatomy of a crochet hook

Tip

Hook

Grip

Handle

CROCHET HOOK SIZES	
U.S.	**Metric**
B/1	2.25 mm
C/2	2.75 mm
D/3	3.25 mm
E/4	3.5 mm
F/5	3.75 mm
G/6	4 mm
7	4.5 mm
H/8	5 mm
I/9	5.5 mm
J/10	6 mm
K/10½	6.5 mm
L/11	8 mm
M/13	9 mm
N/15	10 mm
P	15 mm
Q	16 mm
S	19 mm

Source:
www.yarnstandards.com

10

Yarn Needles (also called tapestry needles)—These are very useful for weaving in ends and seaming. They should have a blunt point to avoid splitting the yarn and should have an eye large enough for the yarn that will be threaded through them.

Embroidery Needles—These are smaller needles that are good for weaving in ends of smaller yarns and threads; used when the large eye of a tapestry needle would leave holes in the fabric.

Split Ring Stitch Markers—These are open rings that slide onto crochet stitches.

Ruler—You may use a dressmaker's tape measure, too, but a ruler is our preference for measuring gauge and other parts of a crocheted piece. A gauge tool is also available that has a right angle cutout that allows the stitches and rows of a fabric to be counted easily.

Row Counter or Paper and Pencil—Keep track of which row you've just completed with these handy tools.

Sticky Notes or Magnetic Board with Magnet—Extremely useful tools for keeping your place in a pattern or chart.

Coilless Safety Pins—Unlike a regular safety pin, these are missing the extra loop of wire at the bend, which can trap fibers and snag yarns.

Rustless Straight Pins—These are used for blocking your crocheted fabric. They hold your crocheted piece in place while it's drying on the blocking board.

Blocking Board—Lay out the damp crocheted piece on this board for blocking and drying. It's very helpful if it has a grid or squares to help with straight lines. You can also use the top of a bed.

Spray Bottle—Wet the crocheted piece using a spray bottle containing water, then wrap the piece in a towel to soak up the excess water before blocking. If you prefer, you may use a steam iron to block the crocheted piece. Lay the piece wrong side up. Do not press the iron down on the fabric but, instead, hold it above the fabric and keep it moving.

Scissors—Always keep them sharp and in a safe place.

Hand Lotion—A good cream will keep your hands and cuticles soft. Dry skin will pull at the fibers in yarns. Some hand lotions will stain yarns and feel greasy on your hands. Look for a product that is made with crocheters in mind (see Sewing Expressions, Resources, page 157).

Swift—This clever contraption holds and expands to fit different-size hanks. It spins around as yarn is pulled off to be wound into a center-pull ball.

Center-Pull Ball—Thread the yarn through the guide of a ball winder and secure. Turn the crank and create a ball that pulls from the inside. This ball won't roll around. Handspinners will know of a tool called the *nostepinne*. It does the same job but takes longer, since you're winding the ball by hand. You may also wind a ball around your hand. Wrap a long tail around your thumb, then wrap the yarn around your fingers. The long tail will pull from the center when the ball is complete.

When winding a center-pull ball either by hand or with a ball winder, take care to wind the yarn loosely. If using a ball winder, do not pull the yarn tightly while turning the crank. When you pull the ball off of the winder, the center should not collapse. If it does, it's wound too tightly. Tight balls put stress on the yarn, which causes it to lose resilience. You may wash the yarn, but if you do, do it before crocheting with it or the garment may shrink when the yarn goes back to having its original bounce.

Beads—Beads come in an endless variety of shapes, sizes, and materials. Round and smooth beads, such as pearls, are the most common shape. Some beads have facets, areas that are smooth and flat, just like on a diamond, which reflect light for a glitzy look. Bicone beads have two points, one at each end of the bead.

Teardrops look just like a tear and may be smooth or faceted. Chips are small, irregular-shaped beads. Regardless of the shape of the bead, its size is determined by measuring its diameter in millimeters (mm). Our favorite beads are made of crystal, glass, and natural materials such as stone and wood. Holes that are drilled into beads can be different diameters, too. This is important to remember when pairing beads with yarn or thread. Make sure to choose a stringing material that will comfortably fit through the bead hole.

Stringing Materials—Choose stringing materials that work well with the diameter of the beads you are using and are strong enough for the weight of the beads. Examples are clear nylon cord or transite, beading wire, silk cord, and nylon or silk thread.

Jeweler's Glue—This is a contact cement with a fine-tip applicator at the end of the tube. It is easy to find in beading shops and is very useful for securing knots. Just apply a drop of the glue to the cut end of your beading thread or cord, and allow it to dry. Clear nail polish may also be used, but we've found it to gum up and discolor some yarns. We've also tried some of the quick-dry gel glues, but they damaged the finish of some beads. You want your pieces to be secure and look great. Jeweler's glue is a tried-and-true friend.

Flexible Twisted Wire Beading Needle—The eye of this beading needle collapses when beads pass over it. The wire bends and is very flexible.

#10 Rigid Beading Needle—This type of needle does not bend. It is good for stringing small beads with thread.

Pliers—For crocheted jewelry, you may want to invest in tools such as chain-nose pliers and round-nose pliers for working with wire findings.

13

Jewelry Findings—A few of the components that give a jewelry piece its structure are earring wires, clasps, and knot covers.

Earring Wires—These are, of course, used to make earrings. Popular styles are the fishhook and leverback hinged.

Clasps—The ends of a necklace or bracelet are connected together with these. Popular styles of clasps are the toggle, box, and magnetic.

Knot Covers (also called bead tips)—Use these at the end of a jewelry piece to hide a knot.

Shaken or Stirred? Mixing a *Yarn Cocktails* Design Properly

Now that you have the right tools, it's time to talk about mixers, the yummy yarns with which you will make your *Yarn Cocktails* design. For best results, use the yarns shown in the photograph and listed in the instructions for each project. If you must substitute a different yarn, be sure to choose one with similar gauge and fiber properties. For example, if you crochet a skirt that calls for a wool yarn and you use cotton instead, your skirt will droop after a while; it won't hug your sexy curves. Why? Because cotton is not an elastic fiber: it doesn't bounce back to hold its shape. Wool's crimp makes it naturally elastic, thus wool is a better choice for a skirt, which needs to be flexible.

It's also important to consider yarn texture. If you are working on a *Yarn Cocktails* design with a basketweave pattern and you substitute a furry yarn for a smooth-textured yarn, the fur will obscure the stitch detail—and all of your hard work.

14

YARN SUBSTITUTIONS GUIDE—STANDARD YARN WEIGHT SYSTEM

Categories of yarn, gauge ranges, and recommended needle and hook sizes.
Use these symbols and descriptions to navigate your way through the abundant
selection of yarns available at your local yarn store. Remember that this chart doesn't
cover yarn texture, so take that into consideration as well when selecting yarn.

Yarn weight symbols and category names	1 Super Fine	2 Fine	3 Light	4 Medium	5 Bulky	6 Super Bulky
Types of yarns in category	sock, fingering, baby	sport, baby	DK, light worsted	worsted, afghan, aran	chunky, craft, rug	bulky, roving
Knit gauge range* in stockinette stitch to 4" (10 cm)	27–32 sts	23–26 sts	21–24 sts	16–20 sts	12–15 sts	6–11 sts
Recommended needle in metric size range	2.25–3.25 mm	3.25–3.75 mm	3.75–4.5 mm	4.5–5.5 mm	5.5–8 mm	8 mm and larger
Recommended needle in U.S. size range	1 to 3	3 to 5	5 to 7	7 to 9	9 to 11	11 and larger
Crochet gauge* ranges in single crochet to 4" (10 cm)	21–32 sts	16–20 sts	12–17 sts	11–14 sts	8–11 sts	5–9 sts
Recommended hook in metric size range	2.25–3.5 mm	3.5–4.5 mm	4.5–5.5 mm	5.5–6.5 mm	6.5–9 mm	9 mm and larger
Recommended hook U.S. size range	B/1 to E/4	E/4 to 7	7 to I/9	I/9 to K/10½	K/10½ to M/13	M/13 and larger

Source: www.yarnstandards.com

*GUIDELINES ONLY: The above reflects the most commonly used
gauges and needle or hook sizes for specific yarn categories.*

Fibers

Need more fiber in your diet? Here are some examples of the many fibers you can choose from. Each fiber has its own unique properties that make it both a challenge and a pleasure to work with. Photos show how the yarn looks by itself and how it looks when crocheted.

Alpaca

Shown: Alpaca with a Twist Big Baby in Autumn Leaves

Properties
- Soft and silky
- Durable and strong
- Lustrous
- Warm—seven times warmer than wool!
- Lighter than wool and drapes beautifully
- Nonallergenic—people who can't wear wool can wear alpaca

Challenges
- Slippery on hook
- Not as crimpy as wool and therefore less elastic

Angora

Shown: Tahki Stacy Charles Jolie in #5023

Properties
- Warm
- Lightweight
- Soft
- Drapes beautifully
- Hydroscopic—wicks moisture away from the body

Challenges
- Inelastic
- May felt if subjected to friction
- Slippery on hook
- A tight crocheter will crush the fiber and won't get a nice halo

Cashmere

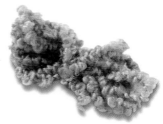

Shown: Fiesta Yarns Tenero in #16101 Abalone

Properties
- Silky soft
- Elastic
- Similar properties as wool

Challenges
- Prone to pilling
- Not durable

Cotton

Shown: Blue Sky Alpacas Dyed Cotton in #602 Honeydew

Properties
- Can be reshaped when wet
- Soft
- Absorbent
- Nonallergenic

Challenges
- Heavy when wet and stretches out of shape
- Prone to pilling

Mohair

Shown: Fiesta Yarns Kokopelli in #3029 Kachina Red

Properties
- Lustrous
- Durable
- Similar to wool

Challenges
- Does not felt as well as wool

Rayon

Shown: Blue Heron Yarns Elephant Chenille in Dusk

Properties
- Acts like a natural fiber
- Very similar to cotton but more absorbent
- Lightweight
- Has breathability
- Drapes well

Challenges
- Will stretch out of shape
- Inelastic
- When wet, it loses great a deal of strength

Silk

Shown: Fiesta Yarns La Luz in Pinon

Properties
- Cultivated silk is lustrous
- Wild silk can be a golden matte
- Very strong
- Drapes beautifully
- Hydroscopic—wicks moisture away from the body, which makes it good for garments that span the seasons

Challenges
- Inelastic
- Unforgiving—shows differences in tension easily
- Will pill

Wool

Shown: Tahki Stacy Charles Soho Tweed in #333

Properties
- Warm
- Elastic
- Hydroscopic—wicks moisture away from the body; wool can absorb up to 40 percent of its weight in water and still feel dry

Challenges
- Some people are allergic to wool
- Depending on the quality, wool may feel very soft or quite harsh and scratchy

Alternative Fibers

Here are some fibers that add interest to your fiber diet.

Corn

Soy

Bamboo

Shown: South West Trading Company Bamboo in Plum

Properties
- Environmentally friendly
- Durable
- Lustrous
- Naturally antibacterial

Challenges
- Yarn may split while crocheting

Shown: Kolláge Yarns Cornucopia in Thai Spice

Properties
- Environmentally friendly
- Easy care, machine washable and dryable
- Durable
- Resilient
- Silky soft
- Drapes beautifully
- Dye won't bleed or fade

Challenges
- Not all colors are available, due to dye techniques

Shown: South West Trading Company Phoenix in Mermaid Mix

Properties
- Environmentally friendly
- Soft
- Lustrous
- Drapes beautifully
- Durable

Challenges
- Inelastic
- Fuzzes with friction

19

Don't Free-Pour; Do a Gauge Swatch!

Gauge swatches are small pieces you crochet first to ensure that your finished project will be the correct size. You won't know if you're using the right tools and mixers without one, and you could end up with a beautiful pair of ruffled panties for yourself that will fit a sumo wrestler perfectly instead. A gauge swatch also determines whether the yarn you choose will produce the gauge that is given for 4" (10 cm); make sure your swatch is larger than 4" (10 cm) square to get a good measurement. The larger the swatch, the more accurate the gauge. We have listed our gauges in simple stitches rather than a more complicated pattern stitch so that it is easier for you to count the number of stitches in an inch (or centimeter).

For your swatch, use as a starting point the hook size listed in the Ingredients section of the pattern. As you crochet more, you may notice that your stitches are consistently tighter or looser than the gauges in patterns. Try swatching with a larger hook if you have more stitches per inch (or centimeter) than the gauge requires. On the other hand, if you don't have enough

stitches per inch (or centimeter) in your swatch, a smaller hook might do the trick. You can also adjust your tension by how you hold the yarn (such as by wrapping it around your little finger), or, if you must, switch to a different yarn.

Once you've crocheted your gauge swatch, measure it accurately. Make sure you include half and quarter stitches as you measure. One half stitch per 4" (10 cm) may not seem like much, but if you multiply that, say, by 9 when you crochet a piece to fit a 36" (91.5 cm)

bust, the garment will end up 4½" (11.5 cm) too big! And just because you have the correct gauge at the beginning of a project, don't assume that it will stay that way throughout the project. Continue to check your gauge as you are crocheting. Stressful days at work may cause you to pull more on the yarn, resulting in tighter stitches, or you may work a little looser on the weekends. We can't say it enough, check gauge and check gauge. Don't make a *Yarn Cocktails* pattern you can't enjoy!

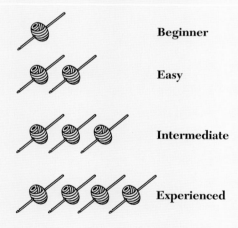

SKILL LEVELS

Not just a garnish, these yarn "olives" indicate each pattern's difficulty level. The more olives you see, the more challenging the project.

Beginner — Projects for first-time crocheters using basic stitches. Minimal shaping.

Easy — Projects using yarn with basic stitches, repetitive stitch patterns, simple color changes, and simple shaping and finishing.

Intermediate — Projects using a variety of techniques, such as basic lace patterns or color patterns, mid-level shaping and finishing.

Experienced — Projects with intricate stitch patterns, techniques, and dimension, such as non-repeating patterns, multicolor techniques, fine threads, small hooks, detailed shaping, and refined finishing.

Source: www.yarnstandards.com

Abbreviations

approx—approximately

beg—beginning

BPdc—back post double crochet

BPdc2tog—back post 2 double crochets together

CC—contrast color

ch(s)—chain(s)

cm—centimeter(s)

dc3Cl—3 double crochet cluster

dc3tog—double crochet 3 sts together

dcdec—double crochet decrease

dc—double crochet

dec—decrease

5dctog—5 double crochets together

FPdc—front post double crochet

FPdc2tog—front post 2 double crochets together

FPhdc—front post half double crochet

FPtr—front post treble crochet

g—gram(s)

hdc—half double crochet

MC—main color

m—meter(s)

mm—millimeter(s)

oz—ounce(s)

pc—popcorn

pm—place marker

rem—remaining, remain(s)

rep—repeat

rnd(s)—round(s)

RS—right side

sc3tog—single crochet 3 sts together

scdec—single crochet decrease

sc—single crochet

sl st—slip stitch

st(s)—stitch(es)

tog—together

tr—treble crochet

4trtog—4 treble crochets together

5trpc—popcorn with 5 treble crochets

6trpc—popcorn with 6 treble crochets

WS—wrong side

yd(s)—yard(s)

yo—yarn over

21

Need a refresher course? See page 148 for a guide to the basics.

Classic Cocktails

22

Keep in Touch with Textured Crochet

Textured crochet is satisfying because it is something that you can do for yourself that cannot be duplicated by a mass-produced, machine-made piece bought in a store. Use texture to express a little bit of your own unique personality. We are sharing two of our favorite textures, the post stitch and the classic, ribbing.

Post stitches look hard, but they are really so easy. What's exciting about post stitches is their adaptability. They can look like ribbing, or they can look like cables. On their own, they play hide-and-seek, popping out, then leaning back, creating an almost musical rhythm. Play post stitches like jazz, and improvise!

A crocheted ribbing sets the tone for your garment. So simple, an undulating textural wave of crocheted ribbing skims the body, flatters without clinging, hugs without constricting. Crocheted ribbing does not just imitate knit ribbing; it has a unique beauty all its own.

We use two methods to create ribbing: working into the back loop of a stitch, and crocheting around the post of a stitch. Usually, you insert the crochet hook through both loops of a stitch. Working into the back loop of a stitch creates a soft rib. Repeating the front post double crochet and the back post double crochet stitches creates a stretchy ribbing.

It's time to create your own "postmodern" world, and get your hooks into these stitches!

LOOPS OF A STITCH

Usually, you work into both loops, but occasionally, a pattern will instruct you to work into the back loop only or the front loop only (see below).

Texture can also be created by working into a stitch while crocheting backward. It's not as complicated as it sounds. The 42nd Street Slippers (shown on page 34) use this method for a fabulous textured look.

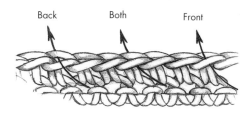

Back   Both   Front

POST PART
OF A STITCH

When you crochet around the tall part of a stitch, known as the post, exciting things start to happen. In addition to ribbing, post stitches can be used to make basketweave and other complicated textures.

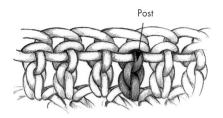

Post

FRONT POST
DOUBLE CROCHET

Yarn over and insert the hook into the fabric from front to back, around the back of the post, and up on the left side of the post. Complete the dc as usual. The dc will sit on the main fabric. When you work a front post double crochet (FPdc), it makes that stitch pop forward because it's sitting on the main fabric.

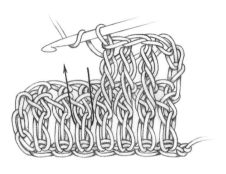

BACK POST
DOUBLE CROCHET

Yarn over and insert the hook into the fabric from back to front, around the front of the post, and down on the left side of the post. Complete the dc as usual. Working a back post double crochet (BPdc) recesses the stitch because it's sitting underneath the main fabric.

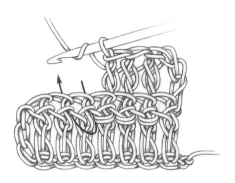

Tip

When crocheting with textured yarns, it helps to feel the stitches with your fingers to determine where to insert your hook.

23

Brandy Alexander Belt

Get your hooks into this waist cincher! Practice the basketweave without distracting shaping in this simple rectangle. A stretchy wool yarn and button closures ensure a perfect fit. Stunning with a simple black dress or equally at home with slacks, this belt will weave its magic on any outfit. Spellbinding!

REFRESH
Front and back posts
(page 23)

Finished Size

3" (7.5 cm) wide × 25 (27½, 29, 31, 33)"
[63.5 (70, 73.5, 78.5, 84) cm] long
Size shown: 25" (63.5 cm) long

Ingredients

210 yds (192 m) light-weight multi-color wool/nylon-blend yarn (3)

Size B/1 (2.25 mm) crochet hook, or size to obtain gauge

Two 1" (2.5 cm) toggle-style buttons in coordinating color

Tapestry needle

Sewing thread in coordinating color

Shown: Fiesta Yarns Socorro (82% wool, 18% nylon; 210 yds [192 m], 114 g per ball): #27105 Amazon, 1 ball

Gauge

26½ sts = 4" (10 cm) in basketweave
24 rows = 4" (10 cm) in basketweave
Don't free-pour; do a gauge swatch!

24

Begin Belt

Ch 21 sts. Sc in second ch from hook and in each ch across—20 scs rem. Ch 2, turn.

Row 1: FPdc in next 3 sts, *BPdc in next 4 sts, FPdc in next 4 sts*; rep from * to * across, working last FPdc around ch-1 of previous row. Ch 2, turn.

Row 2: BPdc in next 3 sts, *FPdc in next 4 sts, BPdc in next 4 sts*; rep from * to * across, working last BPdc around ch-2 of previous row. Ch 2, turn.

Rows 3–4: Rep row 1.

Row 5: Rep row 2.

Row 6: Rep row 1.

Rep rows 1–6 until belt measures 25 (27½, 29, 31, 33)" [63.5 (70, 73.5, 78.5, 84) cm] long, or desired length. Do not fasten off yarn, ch 1, turn at end of last row.

Create button loops: Sl st in first 6 sts, ch 10, sl st in next st to create loop, sl st in next 7 sts, ch 10, sl st in next st to create loop, sl st in next 4 sts, sl st in top of ch-2. Fasten off.

Finishing

Sew buttons to corresponding location of button loops on opposite end of belt, about ½" (1.3 cm) from edge. Weave in all ends.

Classic Sidecar Hat

ad hair day? No one will ever know when you wear this hat! Post stitches and luscious alpaca yarn create a texture that begs to be touched, and the ribbed edge provides the perfect counterpoint. Work this hat from side to side, then stitch up the back seam for instant gratification.

REFRESH
Front and back posts (page 23)
Loops of a stitch (page 22)

Finished Size
Circumference: 20" (51 cm)

Ingredients
82 yds (75 m) bulky-weight alpaca yarn in rust (MC) 5

45 yds (41 m) bulky-weight alpaca yarn in gold (CC) 5

Size K/10½ (6.5 mm) crochet hook, or size to obtain gauge

Tapestry needle

Shown: Alpaca with a Twist Big Baby (100% baby alpaca; 82 yds [75 m] per 100 g ball): #5003 Autumn Leaves (MC), 1 ball; #5004 Summer Squash (CC), 1 ball

Gauge
9 sts = 4" (10 cm) in dc
6 rows = 4" (10 cm) in dc
Don't free-pour; do a gauge swatch!

27

Ribbing

Using MC, ch 6. Sc in second ch from hook and each ch across—5 sc rem. Ch 1, turn.

Row 1: Sc in back loop only across. Ch 1, turn.

Rep row 1 for a total of 54 rows.

Turn clockwise. Working into the long side edge, sc into each row of sc across—54 sc rem. Attach CC, ch 2 (counts as first st in next row) with CC, turn.

Crown

Row 1: Using CC, dc into next 3 sts, *FPdc into next st, dc into next 8 sts*; rep from * to * 4 times more, FPdc into next st, dc into next 4 sts. Ch 2, turn.

Row 2: FPdc into next 3 sts, *BPdc into next st, FPdc into next 8 sts*; rep from * to * 4 times more, BPdc into next st, FPdc into next 3 sts, dc into top of ch-2. Change to MC, ch 2 with MC, turn.

Row 3 (Decrease Row): Dc into next 2 sts, *dcdec, working dc into first part of dec and FPdc into second part of dec, dc into next 7 sts*; rep from * to * 4 times more, dcdec, dc into next 3 sts, dc into top of ch-2—48 sts rem. Ch 2, turn.

Note: Beg with row 4 of the crown, when working the second part of dcdec, be sure to work the specified st (FPdc or BPdc) around *both* stitches of previous decrease.

Row 4 (Decrease Row): FPdc into next 2 sts, *dcdec, working FPdc into first part of dec and BPdc into second part of dec (make sure to work BPdc around both sts of previous decrease), FPdc into next 6 sts*; rep from * to * 4 times more, dcdec, FPdc into next 2 sts, dc into top of ch-2—42 sts rem. Change to CC, ch 2 with CC, turn.

Row 5 (Decrease Row): Dc into next st, *dcdec, working dc into first part of dec and FPdc into second part of dec, dc into next 5 sts*; rep from * to * 4 times more, dcdec, dc into next 2 sts, dc into top of ch-2—36 sts rem. Ch 2, turn.

Row 6 (Decrease Row): Dc into next st, *dcdec, working FPdc into first part of dec and BPdc into second part of dec (make sure to work BPdc around both sts of previous decrease), FPdc into next 4 sts*; rep from * to * 4 times more, dcdec, FPdc, dc into top of ch-2—30 sts rem. Change to MC, ch 2 with MC, turn.

Row 7 (Decrease Row): *Dcdec, working dc into first part of dec and FPdc into second part of dec (make sure to work BPdc around both sts of previous decrease), dc into next 3 sts*; rep from * to * 4 times more, dcdec, dc, dc into top of ch-2—24 sts rem. Ch 2, turn.

Tips

- When picking up stitches on long side edge of ribbing, be sure to pick up through the tighter loops, rather than the looser loops, for a crisper edge.

- When changing colors for the stripes, make sure to carry yarns loosely up the back of the work. Carrying the yarns up too tightly will cause the fabric to pucker and distort.

- Carefully seam the hat together so the seaming yarn doesn't show through.

Row 8 (Decrease Row): *Dcdec, working FPdc into first part of dec and BPdc into second part of dec (make sure to work BPdc around both sts of previous decrease), FPdc into next 2 sts*, rep from * to * 4 times more, dcdec, dc into top of ch-2—18 sts rem. Change to CC, ch 2 with CC, turn.

Row 9 (Decrease Row): FPdc, *dc, dcdec, working dc into first part of dec and FPdc into second part of dec (make sure to work BPdc around both sts of previous decrease)*; rep from * to * 4 times more, dc into top of ch-2—13 sts rem. Ch 2, turn.

Row 10 (Decrease Row): BPdc, *dcdec, working FPdc into first part of dec and BPdc into second part of dec (make sure to work BPdc around both sts of previous decrease)*; rep from * to * 4 times more, dc into top of ch-2—8 sts rem. Ch 1, turn.

Row 11 (Decrease Row): Scdec across, making sure to work scs around both sts of previous decreases—4 sts rem. Fasten off, leaving 18" (45.5 cm) yarn tail for sewing seam.

Finishing

Use woven seam method (see page 156) to sew edges of hat together, beg at top of crown and work down the ribbing. Weave in ends to WS.

Bourbon and Cola Skirt

Perfect for the office, professional finishing makes this skirt eligible for a promotion. A hidden casing for the elastic waistband ensures a comfortable fit, and a deep front post double crochet edging adds texture and a lovely scallop effect to the bottom of the skirt. Executive sweet!

REFRESH

Back loop only (page 22)
Front and back posts (page 23)

Finished Size

XSmall (Small, Medium, Large, XLarge)
Hip circumference: 34 (37, 40, 43, 46)" [86.5 (94, 101.5, 109, 117) cm]
Size shown: Small—37" (94 cm)

Ingredients

975 (1050, 1130, 1255, 1345) yds [875 (960, 1033, 1148, 1230) m] medium-weight wool yarn (4)

Size H/8 (5 mm) crochet hook, or size to obtain gauge

1½ yds (1.4 m) elastic, ½" (1.3 cm) wide

Sewing needle and matching thread

Tapestry needle

Shown: Cascade Yarns Madil Iceland (100% pure virgin wool; 137 yds (125 m) per 100 g ball): #416 Camel, 8 (8, 9, 10, 10) balls

Gauge

14 sc = 4" (10 cm)
18 rows = 4" (10 cm)
Don't free-pour; do a guage swatch!

Stitch Explanation

FPhdc—yarn over hook, insert hook around post of a stitch as for FPdc, yarn over hook and pull up loop, yarn over hook and pull through all 3 loops on hook

Skirt Panel (Make 2)

Waistband

Row 1 (RS): Ch 61 (66, 71, 76, 81), sc into 2nd ch from hook and in each ch across—60 (65, 70, 75, 80) sc rem. Ch 3, turn.

Row 2: Dc in each sc across. Ch 1, turn.

Row 3: Sc into back loop only in each dc across. Ch 1, turn.

Rows 4 and 5: Sc into both loops in each sc across.

Row 6: Fold piece in half length-wise along row 3 with WS facing each other and the dc in row 2 facing you. Ch 1, sc first free loop of beg ch (front half) and front loop only of first st of back half. Matching st for st, continue sc the two halves tog to create tube for elastic. Ch 1, turn.

Body

Row 1 (RS): Sc in each sc across— 60 (65, 70, 75, 80) sc rem. Ch 1, turn.

Rows 2–50: Sc in each sc across. Piece should measure 12" (30.5 cm) from beg. Ch 2, turn.

Scallops

Row 1 (RS): Hdc across. Ch 2, turn.

Row 2: Hdc across. Ch 2, turn.

Row 3: *Hdc in next 4 sts, FPhdc around the hdc 2 rows below the next hdc, skip hdc behind the FPhdc*; rep from * to * across ending with FPhdc around final hdc. Ch 2, turn.

Row 4: Hdc across. Ch 2, turn.

Row 5: *Hdc in next 4 sts, FPhdc around FPhdc 2 rows below, skip hdc behind the FPhdc*; rep from * to * across ending with FPhdc around the FPhdc 2 rows below. Ch 2, turn.

Rows 6–29: Rep rows 4 and 5. Piece should measure 9" (23 cm) from beg of scallops. Fasten off.

Finishing

Use a woven seam (see page 156) to sew side seams of the two panels tog, making sure that the last FPhdc in each row stays on top of the fabric to keep the pattern consistent. Weave ends into WS. Cut elastic to fit waist measurement plus 1" (2.5 cm) extra for overlap. Pull elastic through waistband tube by folding the end of the elastic about 1" (2.5 cm) from end, use handle of the crochet hook to push the fold through the tube. Overlap the ends of elastic and sew tog with needle and thread.

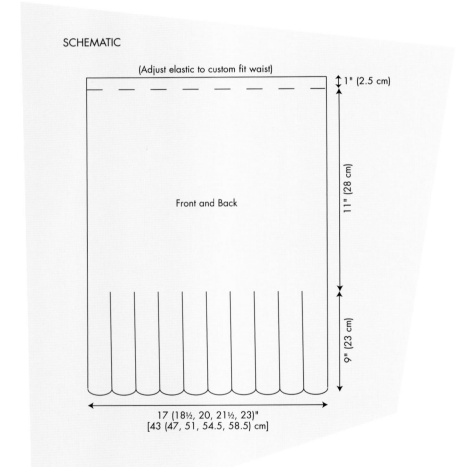

SCHEMATIC

(Adjust elastic to custom fit waist)

1" (2.5 cm)

11" (28 cm)

9" (23 cm)

Front and Back

17 (18½, 20, 21½, 23)"
[43 (47, 51, 54.5, 58.5) cm]

42nd Street Slippers

*S*lip into something comfortable—and luxurious! Reverse Single Crochet, or Crab Stitch, makes a great edging, but here we've used it to make a sideways ribbing by working it in the front loop only of each stitch.

REFRESH
Front loop only, back loop only (page 22)

Finished Size
Small (Medium, Large). Women's U.S. shoe sizes 5/6 (7/8, 9/10) [UK sizes 3 (5, 7)]
Length from heel to toe: 9 (9¾, 10¾)" [23 (25, 27.5) cm]
Width, at widest part: 3¾ (4, 4¼)" [9.5 (10, 11) cm]
Size shown: Small—5/6

Ingredients
260 yds (238 m) medium-weight mohair/wool-blend yarn (A) 4

140 yds (128 m) bulky-weight cashmere/merino wool/polyamide-blend bouclé yarn (B) 5

Size G/6 (4 mm) crochet hook, or size to obtain gauge

Size H/8 (5 mm) crochet hook, or size to obtain gauge

1 pair flip-flops, or 2 (2, 4) sheets 6 mm-thick craft foam

Foam glue (only if using craft foam)

Tapestry needle

Shown: Fiesta Yarns Kokopelli (60% mohair, 40% wool; 130 yds [119 m] per 4 oz hank): #3029 Kachina Red (A), 2 hanks; Tenero (84% cashmere, 12% merino wool, 4% polyamide; 70 yds [64 m] per 2 oz hank): #16101 Abalone (B), 2 hanks; Darice Foamies Extra Firm! Super Thick craft foam; Aleene's FunCraft Foam Glue

Gauge
14 sts, 12 rows = 4" (10 cm) in sc with yarn B and larger hook
16 sts, 19 rows = 4" (10 cm) in sc with yarn A and smaller hook
Note: Yarn B is worked at a firmer gauge than normal, for strength and durability.
Don't free-pour; do a gauge swatch!

Stitch Explanation
Reverse Single Crochet (Crab Stitch)

Step 1
Working from left to right, with hook facing downward, insert hook into stitch to the right of hook.

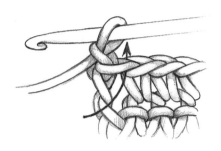

Step 2
Yarn over and pull loop through the stitch loops twisting the hook to face upward at the same time. There will be 2 loops on the hook.

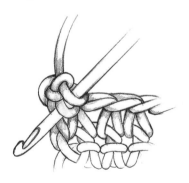

Step 3
Yarn over and draw through both loops on hook.

Step 4
One reverse sc stitch is complete. Rep from Step 1 for next stitch.

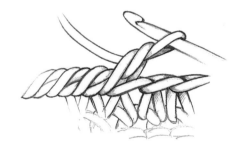

Inside Sole (Make 2)

Row 1: With yarn B and larger hook, ch 9, sc into 2nd ch from hook and in each ch across—8 sc rem. Ch 1, turn.

Rows 2 and 3: Sc across. Ch 1, turn.

Row 4: 2 sc in first sc, 6 sc, 2 sc in last sc—10 sts rem. Ch 1, turn.

Rows 5 and 6: Rep row 2.

Row 7: 2 sc in first sc, 8 sc, 2 sc in last sc—12 sts rem. Ch 1, turn.

Rows 8–12: Rep row 2.

Row 13: 2 sc in first sc, 10 sc, 2 sc in last sc—14 sts rem. Ch 1, turn.

Rows 14–16: Rep row 2.

Row 17: 2 sc in first sc, 12 sc, 2 sc in last sc—16 sts rem. Ch 1, turn.

Rows 18–22: Rep row 2.

For Size Medium Only:

Rows 23–25: Rep row 2.

For Size Large Only:

Rows 23–28: Rep row 2.

Decrease for Toes

Row 1: Scdec, 12 sc, scdec—14 sts rem. Ch 1, turn.

Row 2: Sc across. Ch 1, turn.

Row 3: Scdec, 10 sc, scdec—12 sts rem. Ch 1, turn.

Row 4: Scdec, 8 sc, scdec—10 sts rem. Ch 1, turn.

Row 5: Scdec, 6 sc, scdec—8 sts. Ch 1, turn.

Row 6: Scdec, 4 sc, scdec—6 sts rem.

   Fasten off.

Outside Sole (Make 2)

Row 1: With yarn A and smaller hook, ch 11, sc into 2nd ch from hook and in each ch across—10 sc rem. Ch 1, turn.

Rows 2 and 3: Sc across. Ch 1, turn.

Row 4: 2 sc in 1st sc, 8 sc, 2 sc in last sc—12 sc rem. Ch 1, turn.

Rows 5 and 6: Rep row 2.

Row 7: 2 sc in 1st sc, 10 sc, 2 sc in last sc—14 sc rem. Ch 1, turn.

Rows 8–19: Rep row 2.

Row 20: 2 sc in 1st sc, 12 sc, 2 sc in last sc—16 sc rem. Ch 1, turn.

Rows 21–28: Rep row 2.

Row 29: 2 sc in first sc, 14 sc, 2 sc in last sc—18 sc rem. Ch 1, turn.

Rows 30–34: Rep row 2.

For Size Medium Only:

Rows 35–37: Rep row 2.

For Size Large Only:

Rows 35–40: Rep row 2.

Decrease for Toes

Row 1: Scdec, 14 sc, scdec—16 sts rem. Ch 1, turn.

Row 2: Sc across. Ch 1, turn.

Row 3: Scdec, 12 sc, scdec—14 sts rem. Ch 1, turn.

Row 4: Rep row 2.

Row 5: Scdec, 10 sc, scdec—12 sts rem. Ch 1, turn.

Row 6: Scdec, 8 sc, scdec—10 sts rem. Ch 1, turn.

Row 7: Scdec, 6 sc, scdec—8 sts rem. Ch 1, turn.

   Fasten off. Weave in ends.

Exterior Upper (Make 2)

Row 1: With yarn A and smaller hook, ch 28, dc into 4th ch from hook and in each ch across—26 dc rem. Do not turn.

Row 2: Ch 1, sc into front loop only of last dc made, work in reverse sc by *sc into front loop only of dc to right*; rep from * to *, ending with sl st into top of beg ch-3. Do not turn.

Row 3: Ch 3, dc into back loop only of next st and in each st across. Do not turn.

Rows 4 and 5: Rep rows 2 and 3.

Row 6: Rep row 2.

For Size Medium Only:

Rows 7 and 8: Rep rows 3 and 2 once more.

For Size Large Only:

Rows 7–10: Rep rows 3 and 2 twice more.

Decrease for Toes

Row 1: Ch 3; working in back loop only, dcdec, 21 dc, dcdec in last 2 sts—24 sts rem. Do not turn.

Rows 2, 4, 6, 8, 10, and 12: Ch 1, sc into front loop only of last dc made, work in reverse sc by *sc into front loop only of dc to right*; rep from * to * ending with sl st into top of beg ch-3. Do not turn.

Row 3: Ch 3; working in back loop only, dcdec, 19 dc, dcdec in last 2 sts—22 sts rem. Do not turn.

Row 5: Ch 3; working in back loop only, dcdec, 17 dc, dcdec in last 2 sts—20 sts rem. Do not turn.

Row 7: Ch 3; working in back loop only, dcdec, 15 dc, dcdec in last 2 sts—18 sts rem. Do not turn.

Row 9: Ch 3; working in back loop only, dcdec, 13 dc, dcdec in last 2 sts—16 sts rem. Do not turn.

Row 11: Ch 3; working in back loop only, dcdec, 11 dc, dcdec in last 2 sts—14 sts rem. Do not turn.

Row 13: Ch 3; working in back loop only, dcdec, 9 dc, dcdec in last 2 sts—12 sts rem.

Fasten off.

Interior Upper (Make 2)

Row 1: With yarn B and larger hook, ch 19, sc into 2nd ch from hook and in each ch across—18 sc rem. Ch 1, turn.

Rows 2–9: Sc across. Ch 1, turn.

For Size Medium Only:

Rows 10 and 11: Sc across. Ch 1, turn.

For Size Large Only:

Rows 10–13: Sc across. Ch 1, turn.

Decrease for Toes

Row 1: Scdec, 14 sc, scdec—16 sts rem. Ch 1, turn.

Rows 2, 4, and 6: Sc across. Ch 1, turn.

Row 3: Scdec, 12 sc, scdec—14 sts rem. Ch 1, turn.

Row 5: Scdec, 10 sc, scdec—12 sts rem. Ch 1, turn.

Row 7: Scdec, 8 sc, scdec—10 sts rem.

Fasten off. Weave in ends.

Finishing

If using flip-flops, remove the straps so you're left with only the foam soles. If it's not summer and you don't have any flip-flops, no problem. You can work some magic with craft foam and create your own slipper soles. Either enlarge the template provided (see page 39) on a copy machine and cut out your size, or, using a brown paper grocery bag, place the bag on a hard flat surface, place your foot (or the intended wearer's) on the paper bag, and draw an outline of the foot. Cut around the outline and use it as your template. *Place the template on one sheet of craft foam and trace around it with a pencil. Cut out the foam shape. Rep from * until you have four soles. Note that for sizes Small and Medium, you can get two soles out of each foam sheet. For size Large, more foam sheets are needed because only one fits on each sheet (positioned diagonally). Once you have cut out four foam soles, glue two of them together, taking care to position one on top of the other and match up the edges. Rep for the rem two soles.

Crochet Soles

Place one crocheted outside sole and one crocheted inside sole together, with WS facing. With outside sole facing you, use yarn B and larger hook to sl st these pieces tog at edges. Pause when you've reached three-quarters of the way around. While there is still an opening, insert the flip-flop or double-thick foam cutout, and continue to sl st edges of the pieces tog. Fasten off. Weave in ends. Rep for second set of soles, making sure you insert the flip-flop or foam cutout for the opposite foot.

Place one of the interior upper pieces on one of the soles, making sure the inside sole is facing you, and whip stitch these pieces together, leaving an opening for your foot to slide in.

Place one of the exterior upper pieces over the interior upper piece and work reverse sc through both layers with smaller hook and yarn A at opening for foot. Using yarn A, whip stitch exterior upper piece to slipper around top edge of sole. Weave in ends. Rep for rem slipper.

38

TEMPLATE

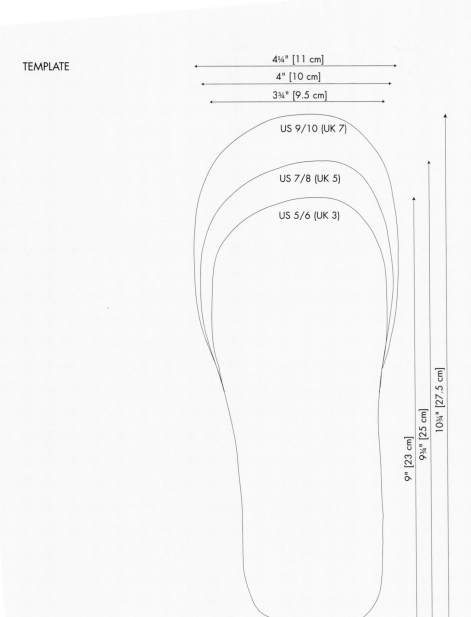

4¼" [11 cm]

4" [10 cm]

3¾" [9.5 cm]

US 9/10 (UK 7)

US 7/8 (UK 5)

US 5/6 (UK 3)

9" [23 cm]

9¾" [25 cm]

10¾" [27.5 cm]

Enlarge template at 200%

Frozen Drinks

Circular Thinking with Crochet in the Round

Once you know how to use a slip stitch to join your chain and create a circle, there's nothing to crocheting in the round. You simply use the same process to join the last stitch to the first stitch of each round. Not only does this enable you to see where each round begins and ends; it creates a series of connected circles instead of a spiral. Once you have worked a round, you will have to choose whether you want your circle to remain flat or if you want it to form a dome shape. A flat circle requires a certain number of increases per row to remain flat; a dome-shaped circle will need fewer increases. Think of it this way—here's a concentric circle:

Of course, it takes more yarn to get around the outside circle than it takes to get around the inside circle. So, it stands to reason that you would need more stitches on the outside, hence the increases. If you only add a few more stitches, the outside stitches push the center up to form the dome. This might be just what you want: a dome-shaped circle makes a lovely hat or bag.

Now, let's say that you want to make a skirt with no seams. Simply chain more stitches before you join to create the circle and you have your tube. Wow, no seams to sew; minimal finishing. Piece of cake!

Place a stitch marker (see Tools of the Trade, page 10) at the beginning of a round if you like to make things easy on yourself. Split ring markers work well for crochet; they have an opening so they slide off the stitch easily.

40

WORKING IN
THE ROUND

Step 1

Most motifs are worked in the round
from the center out. Each round is
worked with the right side always
facing you (that is, the work is never
turned), unless otherwise indicated.
The beginning can be a ring formed
by a number of chains joined together as shown here. For this example,
begin by chaining 5. Insert the hook
into the first of the chains. You want
the right side of the chain facing
you, being careful not to twist the
chain (see the illustration of the
right side of the chain on page 150).

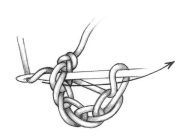

Step 2

Slip stitch into the first chain to join
and form a ring.

Step 3

A turning chain
is made to match
the height of the
stitches to be
worked in the first
round; in this case
chain 3 for a
double crochet
round.

Step 4

Each stitch in round 1 is worked by
inserting the hook into the center
hole of the chain stitch ring.

JOINING IN
THE ROUND

Step 1

Once all of the stitches in a round
are completed, finish the round by
working a slip stitch into the top of
the beginning chain or first stitch.

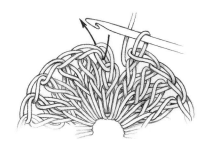

Step 2

The following round is then worked
on top of the previous round. The
round starts with a beginning chain
that matches the height of the stitches to be used in that round. The first
stitch is then usually worked by
inserting the hook through both
loops of the next stitch as shown.

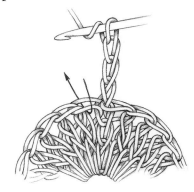

Frozen Mint Necklace, Earrings, and Ring Set

This jewelry set works up fast! Begin crocheting in the morning and wear it out on the town that night. The main part of the necklace is a tube. Just crochet around and around. The metallic yarn is icy with a glimmer of mint. Dress it up with sparkling crystals. The beading is easy because the beads are applied after the tube is finished.

REFRESH
Crochet in the round (page 41)

Finished Size
Necklace: 18" (45.5 cm) long
Earrings: 1¼" (3 cm) long (not including earring wires)
Ring: 1¾ (2, 2⅛)" [4.5 (5, 5.3) cm] ring finger circumference—ring sizes 5 (6, 7)

Ingredients
65 yds (59.5 m) super fine–weight metallic yarn (**1**)

Size B/1 (2.25 mm) crochet hook

54 (3 mm) clear round faceted crystal beads (A)

59 (6 mm) white round faceted crystal beads (B)

60 (4 mm) black bicone crystal beads (C)

1 silver toggle clasp

2 silver earring wires

Size 10 beading needle

Embroidery needle

Jeweler's glue

Shown: For the tube, South West Trading Company Shimmer (50% nylon, 50% polyester; 150 yds [137 m] per 25 g cone): #405 Iridescent, 1 cone; Swarovski 3 mm round faceted crystal, 6 mm round faceted white alabaster, and 4 mm jet hematite bicone crystal beads

Gauge
4 rounds = 1" (2.5 cm)
Don't free-pour; do a gauge swatch!

43

Necklace Tube

Ch 6, sl st into 1st ch to join and form a circle. Pull tail from slip knot forward through center of circle.

Rnd 1: Ch 1, do not turn. Work 6 sc in center of circle. Sl st into beg ch to join—6 sc rem.

Rnd 2: Ch 3, dc in each sc around, sl st into top of beg ch to join.

Rnd 3: Ch 3, dc in each dc around, sl st into top of beg ch-3 to join. Rep rnd 3 until piece measures 18" (45.5 cm) long. Fasten off. Weave in ends.

 *Tips*

- Leave at least a 6" (15 cm) tail when cutting yarn, unless otherwise specified in the pattern.

- Do not tie knots unless specified in the pattern.

- Don't have a stitch marker? Cut a short length of contrasting color yarn and tie it around the stitch.

- If you are using a flexible beading needle, the eye will get flattened by the beads sliding over it. But don't think that you can't use it again. Open the eye of the flexible beading needle with the point of a tapestry needle.

Finishing

Cut a 30" (76 cm) length of yarn and knot it at one end of the tube, leaving a 6" (15 cm) tail.

With beading needle, *slide beads onto the 30" (76 cm) yarn length in this order (B, A, C) twice. Slightly turn the tube. In rnd 3, insert beading needle into the crocheted tube just under one of the dc and then bring it back up*. This anchors the beads to the tube. Rep from * to *, twisting and slightly wrapping the beads around the tube as you go. Continue to the opposite end and knot yarn to tube. Do not cut yarn. Use it to attach one half of the clasp by pulling the yarn through the wire loop on clasp and knotting.

Attach second half of clasp to opposite end of necklace, using the 6" (15 cm) tail. Weave in ends.

Earrings

Work same as for necklace, rep rnd
3 twice more for a total of 5 rnds.

Finishing

Fasten off, leaving a 12" (30.5 cm)
tail. Slip wire loop at base of earring
wire on to the 12" (30.5 cm) tail.
Using embroidery needle, weave tail
into tube to secure earring wire.
Change to beading needle on same
length of yarn and *slide beads on in
this order: B, A, C, B, A, C, B*.
Insert needle into crocheted tube at
rnd 3 and exit at rnd 2 on opposite
side. Rep from * to *, insert needle
into rnd 4. Weave in ends. Apply
jeweler's glue to cut ends.

Rep for second earring, except
begin the first set of beads on the
opposite side of the earring wire so
that the earrings will match.

Ring

Ch 15 (16, 17), sl st into first ch to
join into a circle.
Rnd 1: Ch 1, sc in each ch around,
sl st into ch-1 to join—15 (16, 17) sc.
Rnd 2: Ch 3, dc in each sc around,
sl st into top of beg ch-3 to join.
Rnd 3: Ch 1, sc in each dc, sl st into
ch-1 to join. Fasten off. Weave in
ends.

Finishing

Cut a 12" (30.5 cm) length of yarn.
Using embroidery needle, bring yarn
up through ring fabric. Slide 1 B
bead onto yarn so that it sits on the
RS of fabric. Insert needle down
through fabric. With even yarn tail
lengths, knot the yarn on the WS.
Use the tails to attach 6 C beads,
one at a time, in a circle around the
B bead on the RS. Weave in ends.
Apply jeweler's glue to cut ends.

Floridita Top

f you enjoyed making paper chains in grade school, then you will enjoy making this lively tank. Simple rings interlock to form the edge. Pick up and crochet from them to make a tube that you crochet in the round to the armholes. Raglan shaping and cap sleeves enhance the flattering silhouette, and a wonderfully soft, spongy yarn cradles the body.

REFRESH
Crochet in the round
(page 41)

Finished Size
XSmall (Small, Medium, Large)
31 (35, 39, 44)" [78.5 (89, 99, 112) cm]
Size shown: XSmall—31" (78.5 cm)

Ingredients
300 (345, 390, 435) yds [274 (316, 357, 398) m] multistrand (cotton/viscose/polyamide) bulky-weight yarn in orange (MC) **5**

50 (60, 70, 80) yds [46 (55, 64, 73) m] multistrand (cotton/viscose/polyamide) bulky-weight yarn in yellow (CC) **5**

Size J/10 (6 mm) crochet hook, or size to obtain gauge

Tapestry needle

Shown: Kollàge Yarns Hot Cotton (cotton/viscose/polyester/polyamide; 75 yds [68.5 m] per 59 g ball): Peaches (MC), 4 (5, 6, 6) balls; Sunburst (CC), 1 (1, 1, 2) ball(s)

Gauge
10 sts = 4" (10 cm) in dc
7 rows = 4" (10 cm) in dc
Don't free-pour; do a gauge swatch!

47

Chain-Link Border

First Chain

Using MC, ch 16 sts. Sl st into first ch to form ring, being careful not to twist. Ch 3, 29 dc into ring, sl st into top of ch-3 to join. Fasten off.

Second Chain

Using CC, ch 16 sts. Thread end of ch through center of previous ring, so that it interlocks with previous ring, and sl st into first ch to form ring, being careful not to twist. Ch 3, 29 dc into ring, sl st into top of ch-3 to join. Fasten off. Continue, alternating rings of MC with rings of CC until you have 13 (15, 17, 19) links on your chain.

Last Ring

Place strip of interlocking rings on a flat surface, and arrange so that all the rings lay flat. Fold in half, being careful not to twist. With CC, ch 16 sts. Thread end of ch through center of both end rings, which should be lying on top of each other. Chain should interlock with both these rings. Sl st into first ch to form a ring, being careful not to twist. Ch 3, 29 dc into ring, sl st into top of ch-3 to join. Fasten off. You should now have a tube created by 14 (16, 18, 20) interlocking rings. This is the bottom of the garment.

Body

Rnd 1: Attach MC. Sc into center top 5 dcs of first ring. Now join first ring to second ring: Insert hook into next dc of first ring, yo, draw up a loop (2 loops on hook), then insert hook into dc at top of second ring, yo, draw up a loop (3 loops on hook), yo and draw through all rem loops on hook (scdec to interlock). *Sc into center top 5 dcs of ring, scdec to interlock*; rep from * to * around, sl st into first sc to join. Be very careful not to let the rings twist.

Rnd 2: Ch 3, dc in each st around, sl st into top of ch-3 to join—84 (96, 108, 120) sts rem.

Rep rnd 2 until garment measures 10½ (11, 11½, 12)" [26.5 (28, 29.5, 31) cm] from beg. From here on, you will work back and forth.

Decrease Front

Row 1: Sl st into next 6 sts for right armhole. Ch 3, dc into next 36 (42, 48, 54) sts—37 (43, 49, 55) sts rem. Ch 3, turn.

Row 2: Dcdec, dc to last 3 sts, dcdec, dc into top of ch 3—35 (41, 47, 53) sts rem.
Ch 3, turn.
Rep row 2 until 25 (31, 35, 39) sts rem. Fasten off.

Tips

- Place a split ring marker at beginning of each round to mark the first stitch. You can concentrate on the stitch pattern and let the marker take care of signaling the end of the round.

- One of the great things about crocheting a piece in the round is that you can try it on as you're making it. So, if you want to adjust the length, just add or subtract rows.

Decrease Back

Using MC, work as for front.

Sleeves (Make 2)

Ch 13 (15, 17, 19) sts. Dc into 3 ch from hook and each ch across—11 (13, 15, 17) dc.

Ch 3, turn.

Row 1 (Increase Row): 2 dc into next dc, dc across to last 3 sts, 2 dc into next dc, dc into top of ch 3—13 (15, 17, 19) dc rem.

Ch 3, turn.

Rep row 1 until 23 (25, 29, 33) sts rem. Fasten off.

Finishing

Using woven seam method (page 156), sew raglan sleeves into raglan armholes. Work 1 round sc around each sleeve edge and underarm opening. Work 1 round sc around neckline, skipping every fourth dc of neckline edge. Weave in all ends.

SCHEMATIC

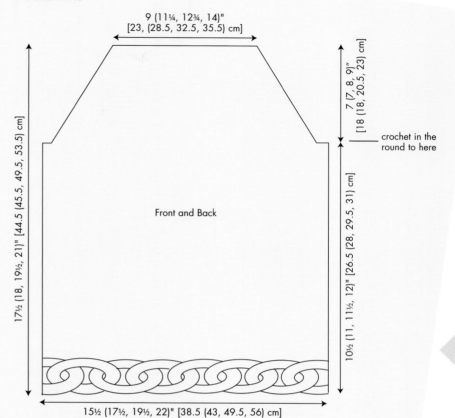

9 (11¼, 12¾, 14)"
[23, (28.5, 32.5, 35.5) cm]

7 (7, 8, 9)"
[18 (18, 20.5, 23) cm]

crochet in the round to here

17½ (18, 19½, 21)" [44.5 (45.5, 49.5, 53.5) cm]

Front and Back

10½ (11, 11½, 12)" [26.5 (28, 29.5, 31) cm]

15½ (17½, 19½, 22)" [38.5 (43, 49.5, 56) cm]

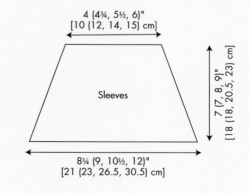

4 (4¾, 5½, 6)"
[10 (12, 14, 15) cm]

Sleeves

7 (7, 8, 9)"
[18 (18, 20.5, 23) cm]

8¼ (9, 10½, 12)"
[21 (23, 26.5, 30.5) cm]

Royal Peach Freeze Top

*W*e've blended lace and light ruffles for a fresh, feminine look. Crochet around and around to create a tube. Attaching the shoulder straps is the only sewing you'll have to do, and they're only an inch (2.5 cm) wide. This pattern lets you try lace and crocheting in the round without overwhelming you with a lot of shaping, too.

REFRESH
Crochet in the round (page 41)

Finished Size
XSmall (Small, Medium, Large, XLarge)
30–32 (34–36, 38–40, 42–44, 46–48)" [76–81.5 (86.5–91.5, 96.5–101.5, 106.5–112, 117–122) cm] chest circumference
Size shown: XSmall—30–32" (76–81.5) cm

Ingredients
712 (750, 900, 1011, 1089) yds [651 (686, 823, 924, 996) m] fine-weight alpaca/silk blend (**2**)

Size E/4 (3.5 mm) crochet hook, or size to obtain gauge

Split ring marker

Tapestry needle

Shown: Blue Sky Alpacas Alpaca Silk (50% alpaca, 50% silk; 146 yds [133 m] per 50 g hank): #136 Champagne, 5 (5, 6, 7, 8) hanks

Gauge
(Sc, 5 dc shell, sc, ch 5) twice = 3" (7.5 cm)
12 dc = 2" (5 cm).
Don't free-pour; do a gauge swatch!

Stitch Explanation
Shell—5 dcs are worked into one st

Note: Slip stitches at the beginning of repeated rounds keep the lace pattern intact. This garment is meant to be close-fitting. The fabric will stretch about 4" (10 cm) in circumference.

50

Body (Lace Panel)

Ch 252 (276, 300, 324, 348), sl st to join into 1st ch and create circle. Be careful not to twist the chain.

Rnd 1: Ch 3, 2 dc in same ch as joining, *skip 2 chs, sc in next ch, ch 5, skip 5 chs, sc in next ch, skip 2 chs, 5 dc in next ch*; rep from * to * 19 (21, 23, 25, 27) times, skip 2 chs, sc in next ch, ch 5, skip 5 chs, sc in next ch, 2 dc into same ch as joining, sl st into top of beg ch 3. Do not turn.

Rnd 2: Ch 1, sc in same st as sl st, *ch 5, sc into ch-5 space, ch 5, sc into 3rd dc of shell*; rep from * to * 19 (21, 23, 25, 27) times, ch 5, sc into ch-5 space, ch 5, sl st into beg sc.

Rnd 3: Sl st into first 2 chs; *sc into ch-5 space, 5 dcs in sc, sc into ch-5 space, ch 5, skip sc*; rep from * to * 20 (22, 24, 26, 28) times, join with sl st into first sc of the round.

Rnd 4: Sl st into 2 dcs, sc into next dc, *ch 5, sc into ch-5 space, ch 5, sc into 3rd dc of shell*; rep from * to * 19 (21, 23, 25, 27) times, ch 5, sc into ch-5 space, ch 5, sl st into first sc of the round.

Rep rnds 3 and 4 until piece measures 6 (6¼, 6½, 6¾, 6¾)" [15 (16, 16.5, 17, 17) cm] from beg, ending with a rnd 4.

Body (Solid Panel)

Setup Rnd: Ch 3, 3 dc in each ch-5 space and 1 dc in each sc around, join with sl st to top of beg ch 3.

Rnd 1: Ch 2, hdc in each dc around, join with sl st to top of beg ch 2.

Rnd 2: Ch 3, dc in each hdc around, join with sl st to top of beg ch 3.

Rep rnds 1 and 2 until piece measures 12 (12½, 13, 13½, 13½)" [30.5 (31.5, 33, 34.5, 34.5) cm] from beg, ending with a rnd 1. Fasten off.

Shoulder Strap (Make 2)

Ch 90 (98, 106, 114, 122).

Row 1: Sc into second ch from hook and in each ch across—89 (97, 105, 113, 121) sts rem. Ch 1, turn.

Row 2: Sc across. Ch 2, turn.

Row 3: 2 dc in first sc, *skip next 3 sc, ch 2, 3 dcs in next sc*; rep from * to * across to last 5 sc, skip next 3 sc, ch 2, 3 dcs in last sc. Ch 2, turn.

Row 4 (RS): *5 dcs in ch-2 space, skip 1 dc, sc in next dc (center dc of the 3 dc shell)*; rep from * to * across. Fasten off, leaving a 12" (30.5 cm) tail for sewing.

Tips

- Always purchase plenty of the same lot number of yarn to complete your project—even one hank or ball more than is listed in the Ingredients section of the pattern. If the extra yarn is not needed, consider saving it in case any repairs need to be made to the piece. You may also use it for coordinating accessories or place it in a basket or bowl for home decor.

- Make sure all the "v"s of the chain are facing you when joining to create circle.

- You can weave ribbon through holes in shoulder straps for an even more feminine look.

52

Bottom Ruffle

Rnd 1: With RS facing and working into free loops of beg ch, attach yarn to any ch-5 space on back side, ch 3, 4 dc in same ch-5 space, 5 dc in free loop of next shell, *5 dc in next ch-5 space, 5 dc in next shell*; rep from * to * around, sl st into top of beg ch 3 to join.

Rnd 2: Ch 2, dc in first dc, 2 dc in each of next 4 dc, ch 2, skip next 5 dc, *2 dc in each of next 5 dc that make up shell, ch 2, skip next 5 dc*; rep from * to * around, sl st into top of beg ch 2 to join.

Rnd 3: Sl st in each of 9 dc to next ch-2 space, (3 sc, sl st) in ch-2 space, *sl st in each dc to next ch-2 space, (3 sc, sl st) in ch-2 space*; rep from * to * around, sl st into first st to join. Fasten off.

Finishing

Place body tube on flat surface and position the sl st joining seam at left or right side and the fasten off at back side. Position shoulder straps approx 2¾ (3, 3½, 3½, 3¾)" [7 (7.5, 9, 9, 9.5) cm] from sides of body. Overlap each strap end inside the body about 1" (2.5 cm), and sew to front and back. Lightly block lace.

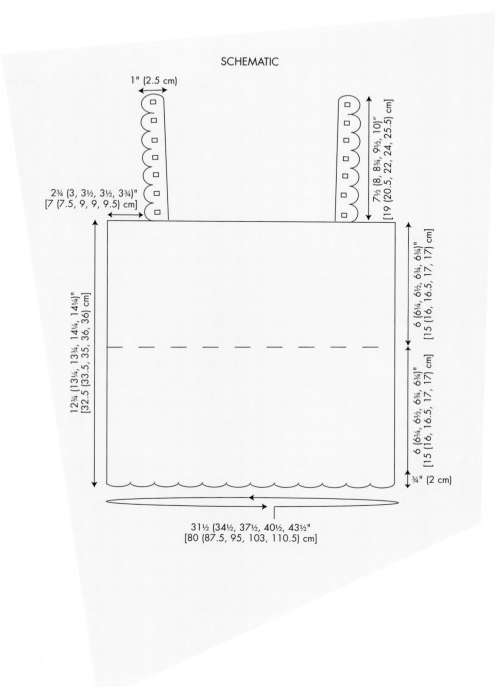

SCHEMATIC

1" (2.5 cm)

7½ (8, 8¾, 9½, 10)" [19 (20.5, 22, 24, 25.5) cm]

2¾ (3, 3½, 3½, 3¾)" [7 (7.5, 9, 9, 9.5) cm]

12¾ (13¼, 13¾, 14¼, 14¼)" [32.5 (33.5, 35, 36, 36) cm]

6 (6¼, 6½, 6¾, 6¾)" [15 (16, 16.5, 17, 17) cm]

6 (6¼, 6½, 6¾, 6¾)" [15 (16, 16.5, 17, 17) cm]

¾" (2 cm)

31½ (34½, 37½, 40½, 43½)" [80 (87.5, 95, 103, 110.5) cm]

Raspberry Margarita Fingerless Gloves

*T*hese fingerless gloves take crocheting in the round to new heights. Once you've crocheted the ribbed edging, everything else is done in the round, including the finger and thumb openings. Make the most out of this tour de force with a buttery-soft cashmere yarn that will caress your fingers as you crochet, and pamper them as you wear these gloves.

REFRESH
Crocheting into the back loop (page 22)
Crocheting in the round (page 41)

Finished Size
4" (10 cm) wide × 6" (15 cm) long

Ingredients
190 yds (173.75 m) super fine–weight 100% cashmere yarn in hand-dyed multicolors

Size 0 (3 mm) steel crochet hook, or size to obtain gauge

Tapestry needle

Shown: Mountain Colors Cashmere (100% cashmere; 95 yds [87 m] per 28.5 g ball): Firestorm, 2 balls

Gauge
24 sts = 4" (10 cm) in sc
32 rows = 4" (10 cm) in sc
Don't free-pour; do a gauge swatch!

Right Glove

Cuff

Ch 11. Sc in back loop of second ch from hook and in each ch across—10 scs. Ch 1, turn.

Rows 2–47: Sc in back loop of each st across. Ch 1, turn.

Join to form tube for wrist: *Insert hook through first sc, then through bottom bump of foundation ch, yo, pull through loops*; rep from * to * across. Turn tube inside out so seam faces inside of tube. Begin working in the round.

Palm

Rnd 1: Ch 1, sc into the end of each row of tube—48 scs. Sl st into first sc to join.

Rnd 2: Ch 1, sc in each st around. Sl st into first sc to join.

Rnd 3: Ch 1, sc in next 35 sts, 2 sc in next sc, sc in next sc, 2 sc in next sc, sc in next 10 sts—50 scs rem. Sl st into first sc to join.

Rnd 4: Ch 1, sc in next 35 sts, 2 sc in next sc, sc in next sc, 2 sc in next sc, sc in next 12 sts—52 scs rem. Sl st into first sc to join.

Rnd 5: Ch 1, sc in next 35 sts, 2 sc in next sc, sc in next sc, 2 sc in next sc, sc in next 14 sts—54 scs rem. Sl st into first sc to join.

Rnds 6–18: Ch 1, sc in each st around. Sl st into first sc to join.

Begin Thumb Opening

Rnd 19: Ch 1, sc in next 21 sts, ch 9, skip next 9 sts, sc in next 24 sts—54 scs rem. Sl st into first sc to join.

Rnd 20: Ch 1, sc in next 20 sts, sc in 9 ch for thumb opening, sc in next 25 sc. Sl st into first sc to join.

Rnds 21–31: Ch 1, sc in each st around. Sl st into first sc to join.

Index Finger

Rnd 1: Ch 1, sc in next 15 sts, ch 4, turn work counterclockwise, sl st in first sc to create index finger opening—19 scs rem.

Rnd 2: Ch 1, sc in next 15 sts, sc in each of next 4 ch, sl st in first sc of index finger rnd 1.

Rnds 3–4: Ch 1, sc in each st of index finger around. Sl st in first st to join.

After rnd 4 is completed, fasten off.

Middle Finger

Rnd 1: Attach yarn at base of 15th st of index finger. Ch 1, sc into next 7 sts, ch 4. Turn work counterclockwise to face other side and sc in 6 scs to the right of the first sc of index finger, sc in each of the bottom bumps at the base of the four chs from index finger. Sl st in first sc to create middle finger opening—21 scs rem.

Rnd 2: Ch 1, sc in next 6 sts, sc in each of next 4 ch, sc in rem 11 scs, sl st in first sc to join.

Rnds 3–4: Ch 1, sc in each st of middle finger around. Sl st in first sc to join.

After rnd 4 is completed, fasten off.

Ring Finger

Rnd 1: Attach yarn at base of seventh st of middle finger. Ch 1, sc into next 7 sts, ch 4. Turn work counterclockwise to face other side and sc in 6 scs to the right of the first sc of middle finger, sc in each of the bottom bumps at the base of the ch-4 from middle finger—21 scs. Sl st in first sc to create ring finger opening.

Rnd 2: Ch 1, sc in next 6 sts, sc in each of next 4 chs, sc in rem 11 scs, sl st in first sc to join.

Rnds 3–4: Ch 1, sc in each st of ring finger around. Sl st in first sc to join.

After rnd 4 is completed, fasten off.

Pinkie

Rnd 1: Attach yarn at base of seventh st of ring finger. Ch 1, sc in 13 sts at end of palm, sc in each of the bottom bumps at the base of the ch-4 from ring finger—17 scs. Sl st in first sc to create pinkie opening.

Rnds 2–4: Ch 1, sc in each st of pinkie around. Sl st in first sc to join.

After rnd 4 is completed, fasten off.

Thumb

Rnd 1: Attach yarn at bottom right of beg of thumb opening. Ch 1, sc in 20 sts around. Sl st in first sc to join.

Rnds 2–4: Ch 1, sc in each st around. Sl st into first sc to join.

After rnd 4 is completed, fasten off.

Weave in all ends.

Left Glove

Work as for right glove to index finger.

Index Finger: Ch 1, sc in next 30 scs, ch 4. Counting back from hook, sl st in 19th st from hook to form index finger opening.

Work remainder of left glove as for right glove. Weave in all ends to WS.

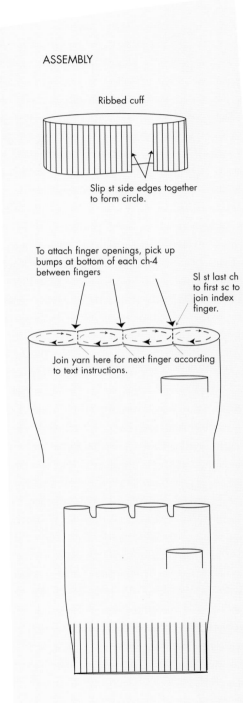

ASSEMBLY

Ribbed cuff

Slip st side edges together to form circle.

To attach finger openings, pick up bumps at bottom of each ch-4 between fingers

Sl st last ch to first sc to join index finger.

Join yarn here for next finger according to text instructions.

Champagne Drinks

Bobbles and Baubles and Plaid—Oh My!

Bobbles, beads, and other embellishments add excitement and interest. It's a small investment that reaps big dividends, adding sophistication to even a beginner project without adding difficulty. Are you ready to give your crochet a makeover? Let's dive right in.

Popcorns and bobbles are very similar to each other. They are both types of cluster stitches: several stitches worked into one stitch or space. With a popcorn, however, each stitch is completed as it is worked, whereas with a bobble, you leave the last loop of each stitch on the hook. As a result, popcorns are a little more subtle, and bobbles have a more rounded shape. Some other cluster stitches are puffs and shells.

POPCORN

To make a popcorn, work several stitches into one stitch, carefully remove the hook from the last loop, insert the hook through the top of the beginning chain or first stitch, and pull the last loop through it to secure.

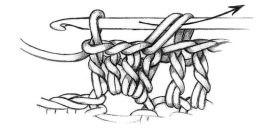

BOBBLE

To make a bobble, work several stitches into one stitch or space, leaving the last loop of each stitch on the hook. After the correct number of stitches is worked into one stitch or space, yarn over the hook and pull through all of the loops on the hook. This gathers up the stitches at the top and creates the rounded shape. The wrong side of the work will face you when creating bobbles.

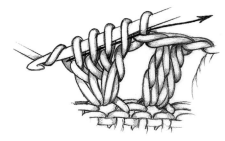

58

BEADS

Beads are exciting by themselves. They come in lots of different materials, textures, shapes, and sizes. Don't be intimidated by the use of beads in your crochet projects. If you've never worked with beads before, our jewelry pieces are a great place to get your feet wet.

There are a variety of ways to add beads to crocheted pieces. You can slide beads directly onto the yarn or thread you're crocheting with. Nylon or silk thread can be used to apply beads to finished fabric, a crochet hook can be used to pull a loop of yarn through the center of the bead, and our favorite— purchase yarn that has the beads already strung and twisted within the fibers. With the beads already on the yarn, the prep work is done for you and you can jump right into crocheting.

PLAID

If you find yourself attracted to colorwork, but aren't quite ready to take on all those bobbins just yet, then crocheted plaid is for you. Crocheted plaid is a surface embellishment created here by single crocheting stripes up a vertical column of ch-2 spaces.

After you have crocheted the main piece, simply take your yarn and hook, and slip stitch into the bottom ch-2 space to anchor the yarn. Insert hook through ch-2 space, yarn around hook, and pull up a loop. Complete as for single crochet. Continue inserting the hook through next ch-2 space directly above the one you just worked, pulling up a loop, and completing single crochets all the way up the column.

When combined with easy horizontal stripes on the main piece, it gives the impression of great complexity with minimal effort, and creates a timeless, classic look.

59

Tips

- Remember, when working sc, insert the hook into the first sc of the row unless otherwise instructed. This applies to sc and sl st. The turning ch does not count as the first st in the row.

- After you complete each bobble, work the next stitch firmly and your bobbles will pop out nicely away from you.

Champagne Polonaise Headband

U se this headband to practice the crocheted plaid technique. It is basically a rectangle; the ends of the headband are tapered with easy decreases and then sewn together. A ribbon yarn consisting of three alternating fibers does the colorwork for you: each fiber takes the dye differently to create a self-striping effect so you only have to use two colors to mimic an intricate plaid pattern. The fiber content of the yarn makes the headband stretchy enough to go over the head. A class act!

REFRESH
Crochet plaid (page 59)

Finished Size
2½" (6.5 cm) at widest point × 18" (45.5 cm) long (before joining ends)

Ingredients
35 yds (32 m) ¼" (6 mm) -wide fine-weight ribbon yarn in reds and pink (MC) **2**

15 yds (13.7 m) ¼" (6 mm) -wide fine-weight ribbon yarn in black (CC) **2**

Size G/6 (4 mm) crochet hook, or size to obtain gauge

Tapestry needle

Shown: Berroco Boho (48% nylon, 25% cotton, 27% rayon; 98 yds [90 m] per 50 g ball): #9272 Torero (MC), 1 ball; #9214 Black Magic (CC), 1 ball

Gauge
18 sts = 4" (10 cm) in sc
23 rows = 4" (10 cm) in sc
Don't free-pour; do a gauge swatch!

60

Headband

Row 1: Using MC, ch 5. Sc in second ch from hook and each ch across—4 scs rem. Ch 1, turn.

Rows 2–11: Sc in each sc across. Ch 1, turn.

Row 12: Sc in each sc across. Ch 4, turn.

Row 13: Sc in second ch from hook, sc in next ch, ch 2, skip third ch, sc in next 4 sc. Ch 4, turn.

Row 14: Sc in second ch from hook, sc in next ch, ch 2, skip third ch, sc in next 4 sc, ch 2, skip ch-2 space, sc in last 2 sc. Ch 1, turn.

Rows 15–19: Sc in next 2 sc, ch 2, skip ch-2 space, sc in next 4 sc, ch 2, skip ch-2 space, sc in next 2 sc. Change to CC. Ch 1, turn.

Rows 20–21: Rep row 15. Change to MC.

Rows 22–27: Rep row 15. Change to CC.

Changing colors same as above, work rows 20–27 five times more, or until headband reaches desired length. After completing row 27 of last rep, do not change to CC; continue with MC as follows:

Decrease to taper edge: Sl st in next 3 sts, ch 1, sc in next 4 scs. Do not work into final 3 sts—4 sts rem. Rep rows 2–12 once more. Fasten off. Weave in all ends.

Plaid

Using CC, join in bottom right ch-2 space with sl st. Working vertically, work sc into next ch-2 space directly above. Continue as above, up to the top edge, always working sc into next ch-2 space directly above previous ch-2 space. Sc into last ch-2 space at top. Fasten off. Rep process on bottom left side, beginning in bottom left ch-2 space and working vertically to top edge.

Finishing

Use woven seam method (see page 156) to sew tapered ends of rectangle together. Weave in any remaining ends.

Ritz Cocktail Bobble Belt

These bobbles will sparkle. This belt is the perfect accessory for a wild night out. It looks great worn inside or outside belt loops. A small crochet hook with this yarn yields a firm fabric.

REFRESH
Bobble (page 58)

Finished Size
1½" (3.8 cm) wide × 30" (76 cm), or desired length

Ingredients
200 yds (183 m) light-weight metallic yarn in gold (3)

Size B/1 (2.25 mm) crochet hook, or size to obtain gauge

Tapestry needle

Shown: Berroco Suede Deluxe (85% nylon, 10% rayon, 5% polyester; 100 yds [92 m] per 50 g ball): #3920 Tonto Gold, 2 balls

Gauge
6 sc = 1" (2.5 cm)

4 rows in sc = ½" (1.3 cm)

Don't free-pour; do a gauge swatch!

Stitch Explanation
5dctog—*yo hook, insert hook into next st, yo hook and pull it up through fabric, yo hook and pull through 2 loops*; rep from * to * 4 times—you will have 6 loops on hook, yo hook and pull through all 6 loops.

Belt
Ch 8, sc in second ch from hook, sc across—7 sc rem. Ch 1, turn.

Row 1: Sc in 2 sc, ch 3, skip 3 chs, sc in 2 sc. Ch 1, turn.

Row 2: Sc in 2 sc, sc in back of each of 3 chs, sc in 2 sc. Ch 1, turn.

Rows 3–8: Sc across. Ch 1, turn.

Row 9 (WS): Sc in first sc, 5dctog in next sc, 3 sc, 5dctog in next sc, sc in last sc. Ch 1, turn.

Row 10: Sc across. Ch 1, turn.

Row 11: 3 sc, 5dctog in next sc, 3 sc. Ch 1, turn.

Row 12: Sc across. Ch 1, turn.

Rep rows 9–12 until piece measures 2½" (6.5 cm) less than desired waist or hip measurement.

Rep row 9 once more.

Work 8 rows of sc.

Bobbles for Closure
Do not ch 1. Turn, sl st in 4 sc, ch 10, 5dctog in 3rd ch from hook. Pull yarn to tighten bobble. Fasten off. Weave in ends to WS.

Finishing
Lightly block the fabric by spraying with water and pinning to the desired dimensions on a blocking board, or block the belt and hold a steam iron above it, keeping the iron moving. Let fabric dry, and the belt is ready to wear.

Champagne Charlie Necktie

*N*ow that you've practiced the plaid technique on a headband, here's a more complicated application. Crocheted with a fine-gauge yarn in subdued, masculine colors, this necktie is the perfect gift. Because the yarn is lightweight and the weave is tight, the necktie is professional enough to wear to the office with a dress shirt and suit. The tie's the limit!

REFRESH
Crocheted plaid
(page 59)

Finished Size
2½" (6.3 cm) at widest point × 53"
(134.5 cm) long

Ingredients

86 yds (78.5 m) super fine–weight wool yarn in blue (A) 🧶**1**

56 yds (51 m) super fine–weight wool yarn in multicolored blues/browns (B) 🧶**1**

30 yds (27.5 m) super fine–weight wool yarn (C) in brown 🧶**1**

Size 6 (1.8 mm) steel crochet hook, or size to obtain gauge

Tapestry needle

Shown: Interlacements Tiny Toes (100% merino wool; 185 yds [169 m] per 50 g ball):
#258 blue (A), 1 ball
#217 multicolor (B), 1 ball
#260 brown (C), 1 ball

Gauge

32 sts = 4" (10 cm) in sc
32 rows = 4" (10 cm) in sc
Don't free-pour; do a gauge swatch!

64

Stripe Pattern

*Rows 1–6: A

Rows 7–8: B

Rows 9–12: A

Rows 13–14: C

Rows 15–16: A

Rows 17–18: C

Rows 19–22: A

Rows 23–24: B

Rep color sequence from * to end of tie.

Front

Using A, ch 16. Sc in second ch from hook, ch 2, skip next ch, sc in next 2 chs, ch 2, skip next ch, sc in next 5 chs, ch 2, skip next ch, sc in next 2 chs, ch 2, skip next ch, sc in next ch— 15 sts rem. Ch 1, turn.

Row 1: Following color sequence as listed under Stripe Pattern above, beginning with row 1, sc in first st, ch 2, skip next ch-2 space, sc in next 2 sts, ch 2, skip next ch-2 space, sc in next 5 sts, ch 2, skip next ch-2 space, sc in next 2 sts, ch 2, skip next ch-2 space, sc in next st. Ch 1, turn.

Rep row 1 until tie measures 11½" (29 cm). Continue to follow Stripe Pattern sequence throughout.

Decrease Section

Row 1: Scdec into sc and ch-2 space, sc in next 2 sts, ch 2, skip next ch-2 space, sc in next 5 sts, ch 2, skip next ch-2 space, sc in next 2 sts, scdec into ch-2 space and sc—13 sts rem. Ch 1, turn.

Rows 2–35: Sc in next 3 sts, ch 2, skip next ch-2 space, sc in next 5 sts, ch 2, skip next ch-2 space, sc in next 3 sts. Ch 1, turn.

Row 36: Scdec, sc in next st, ch 2, skip next ch-2 space, sc in next 5 sts, ch 2, skip next ch-2 space, sc in next st, scdec—11 sts rem. Ch 1, turn.

Rows 37–70: Sc in next 2 sts, ch 2, skip next ch-2 space, sc in next 5 sts, ch 2, skip next ch-2 space, sc in next 2 sts. Ch 1, turn.

Row 71: Scdec, ch 2, skip next ch-2 space, sc in next 5 sts, ch 2, skip next ch-2 space, scdec—9 sts rem. Ch 1, turn.

Rows 72–89: Sc in next st, ch 2, skip next ch-2 space, sc in next 5 sts, ch 2, skip next ch-2 space, sc in next st. Ch 1, turn.

Row 90: Sc in next st, ch 2, skip next ch-2 space, scdec, sc in next st, scdec, ch 2, skip next ch-2 space, sc in next st—7 sts rem. Ch 1, turn.

Row 91: Sc in next st, ch 2, skip next ch-2 space, sc in next 3 sts, ch 2, skip next ch-2 space, sc in next st. Ch 1, turn.

Rep row 91 until tie measures 37½" (95 cm) from beg. Continue Stripe Pattern sequence throughout.

Increase Section

Row 1: 2 scs in next st, ch 2, skip next ch-2 space, sc in next 3 sts, ch 2, skip next ch-2 space, 2 scs in next st—9 sts rem. Ch 1, turn.

Rows 2–31: Sc in next 2 sts, ch 2, skip next ch-2 space, sc in next 3 sts, ch 2, skip next ch-2 space, sc in next 2 sts. Ch 1, turn.

Row 32: 2 scs in next st, sc in next st, ch 2, skip next ch-2 space, sc in next 3 sts, ch 2, skip next ch-2 space, sc in next st, 2 scs in next st—11 sts rem. Ch 1, turn.

Rows 33–62: Sc in next 3 sts, ch 2, skip next ch-2 space, sc in next 3 sts, ch 2, skip next ch-2 space, sc in next 3 sts. Ch 1, turn.

Row 63: Sc in next st, ch 2, sc in next 2 sts, ch 2, skip next ch-2 space, sc in next 3 sts, ch 2, skip next ch-2 space, sc in next 2 sts, ch 2, sc in next st—13 sts rem. Ch 1, turn.

Row 64: Sc in next st, ch 2, skip next ch-2 space, sc in next 2 sts, ch 2, skip next ch-2 space, sc in next 3 sts, ch 2, skip next ch-2 space, sc in next 2 sts, ch 2, skip next ch-2 space, sc in next st. Ch 1, turn.

Rep row 64 until tie measures 53" (134 cm) from beg. Fasten off.

Plaid

Using B, join in bottom right ch-2 space of tie front with sl st. Working vertically, work sc into next ch-2 space directly above. Continue as above, always working sc into next ch-2 space directly above up to top edge where scdec occurs. Sc into last ch-2 space, fasten off. Rep process on bottom left side of tie front, beginning in bottom left ch-2 space and working vertically to last ch-2 space. Rep process on bottom right and bottom left of other end of tie. Using C, rep process on remaining two columns of ch-2 spaces that are located in the bottom center each side of the 5 sc, working plaid vertically from one end of tie to the other.

Finishing

Weave in all ends to WS with tapestry needle. Block to measurements.

SCHEMATIC

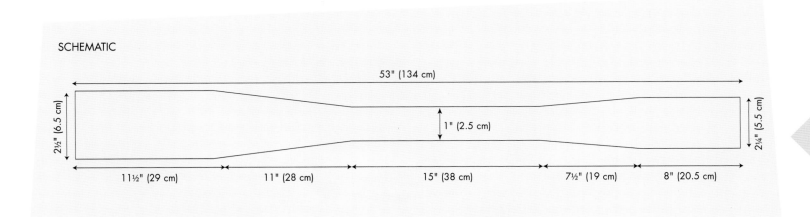

53" (134 cm)

2½" (6.5 cm)

1" (2.5 cm)

2¼" (5.5 cm)

11½" (29 cm)   11" (28 cm)   15" (38 cm)   7½" (19 cm)   8" (20.5 cm)

67

Mimosa Necklace and Bracelet Set

*C*reate your own beads by making bobbles. For the necklace, crochet each bobble separately. Then, string them onto nylon beading cord along with pearls and crystals. The bracelet is fashioned with continuous bobbles wrapped with pearls. This set looks more complicated than it is—just 3 stitches.

REFRESH
Bobble (page 58)

Finished Size

Necklace length: 18" (45.5 cm) outer strand, 14" (35.5 cm) inner strand
Bracelet: 7" (18 cm)

Ingredients

50 yds (45.7 m) medium-weight silk yarn with crystal beads (4)

Size F/5 (3.75 mm) crochet hook, or size to obtain gauge

45 (6 mm) gold pearls

51 (6 mm) peach pearls

20 (4 mm) peach pearls

24 (4 mm) gold pearls

15 (4 mm) light peach round crystals

18 (3 mm) light topaz round crystals

4 clear seed beads

4 gold knot covers

1 large gold filigree round box clasp, 2-strand (for necklace)

1 small gold filigree round box clasp (for bracelet)

Size 10 beading needle

Flexible beading needle

5 yds (4.5 m) tan nylon beading thread, size D

2 yds (2 m) clear nylon beading cord

Needle-nose or chain-nose pliers

Jeweler's glue

Shown: Tilli Tomas Mariel's Crystals (100% spun silk with Swarovski crystals; 120 yds [110 m] per hank): Natural, 1 hank; Swarovski 6 mm pearls in peach and bright gold, 4 mm pearls in peach and bright gold, 4 mm light peach round crystal, 3 mm light Colorado topaz round crystal; Fire Mountain Gems gold filigree round box clasps and light tan nylon beading thread

Gauge

2 (4trtog) = 1½" (4 cm) for bracelet
1 bobble = ½" (1.3 cm) for necklace
Don't free-pour; do a gauge swatch!

Stitch Explanation

4trtog—*yo hook twice, insert hook into ch, draw up loop, (yo hook and pull through 2 loops on hook) twice*; rep from * to * leaving one more loop on hook with each tr; when 5 loops are on hook, yo hook and pull through all 5 loops and gather.

69

Necklace

Bobble Bead (Make 26)

Ch 4, 4trtog into fourth ch from hook. Sl st into same ch to create a ball shape. Fasten off. Knot the beg and ending yarn tails tog. Weave in ends.

Outer Strand

Prepare one end of the necklace by cutting a 36" (91.5 cm) length of nylon beading cord. Tie a surgeon's knot about 3" (7.5 cm) from end by first tying an overhand knot, wrapping the right end of cord around the left one several times.

Then, tie a regular overhand knot with the left cord over the right.

Pull tightly.

With flexible beading needle, slide on one clear seed bead, inserting needle through bead again as shown.

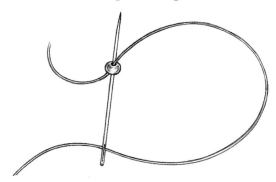

This will lock the bead in place when you slide it to the knot.

Slide on one knot cover as shown.

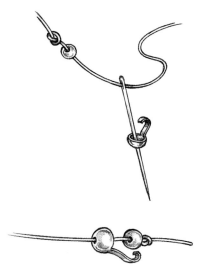

Trim nylon cord and place jeweler's glue on cut end to prevent the knot from coming out. Do not close knot cover.

*Slide on 1 (6 mm) peach pearl. Slide on 1 (6 mm) gold pearl. Slide on 1 (6 mm) peach pearl. Slide on 1 bobble bead, inserting needle through its center. Slide on 1 (6 mm) gold pearl. Slide on 1 (6 mm) peach pearl. Slide on 1 (6 mm) gold pearl.

Slide on 1 bobble bead, inserting
needle through its center*. Rep
from * to * 7 times more, then finish as follows:

Slide on 1 more (6 mm) peach pearl.
Slide on 1 (6 mm) gold pearl.
Slide on 1 more (6 mm) peach pearl.
Slide on another knot cover with
needle inserted in opposite direction from before (see below). Slide
on a clear seed bead and insert
needle through the bead again (see
previous page). Move seed bead and
knot cover next to the last peach
pearl. Knot the clear nylon cord.
Trim cord and apply jeweler's glue
to the cut end. Close the knot covers around the top jump rings on
clasp, using needle-nose or chain-
nose pliers. This will allow the
strand to rest on the outside.

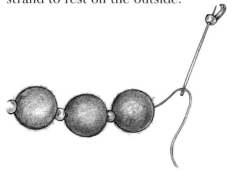

71

Inner Strand

Rep the steps for preparing the end as in the beginning of the outer strand instructions, cutting 20" (51 cm) length of nylon beading cord for the inner strand.

Slide on beads and bobbles in this order:

*(4 mm gold pearl, 3 mm light topaz) 3 times; 4 mm gold pearl **; 1 Bobble Bead; (4 mm peach pearl, 4 mm light peach round crystal) 3 times; 4 mm peach pearl; 1 Bobble Bead*.

Rep from * to * 4 times more.

Rep from * to ** once.

Rep the steps for attaching the final knot cover as in the outer strand, but close the knot covers for the inner strand around the bottom jump rings of the clasp so that this strand will rest inside the outer strand.

Bracelet

Ch 4, 4trtog into fourth ch from hook.
Ch 5, 4trtog into fourth ch from hook.
Rep from * to * 6 times more.
Fasten off.

Onto a 12" (30.5 cm) length of nylon beading thread and using size 10 beading needle, slide on 5 (6 mm) peach pearls. Form a circle of pearls around one end of first bobble and sew the pearls to the bobble fabric so they won't interfere with the clasp. Tie the ends of the beading thread in a surgeon's knot. Rep from * to * in this order:

Slide on 5 (6 mm) gold pearls, wrap the pearls around the ch between 2 bobbles, tie ends tog. Slide on 5 peach pearls, wrap the pearls around the ch between 2 bobbles, tie ends tog; rep from ** to ** 3 times more, wrapping the last 5 peach pearls around the end of the last bobble and sew to bobble fabric same as beg 5 pearls.

Trim beading thread. Apply jeweler's glue to the knots. Insert tail from slip knot into the jump ring at one end of clasp. Tie surgeon's knot. Weave yarn end into bobble. Rep for other end of bracelet.

Tips

- For added strength and security at the clasps, insert the beading needle back through beads close to knot cover and tie a couple of knots to the nearest bobble fabric.

- Scissors with sharply pointed tips will allow you to trim the nylon thread closely with ease.

- Placing beads in a container or on a felt pad will help keep them from spilling and rolling everywhere while you create.

73

Tropical Drinks

A Cute Angle

When you increase or decrease in crochet, you are not just adding and subtracting stitches, you are also shaping a fabric. Increases and decreases create contours to improve the fit of a garment; they can also be manipulated to create angles and exciting stitch patterns.

One decrease we like is the versatile dc3tog decrease. We've created anything from ruffles to waves with this decrease.

Here's how to work a dc3tog: *yo and insert hook into next st, yo hook and draw up loop, yo and pull through first 2 loops on hook*; rep from * to * 2 more times; there will be 4 loops on hook; yo and pull through all 4 loops on hook.

When you strategically place decreases, and work them every row, you create a mitered angle in your crocheted fabric. And that's just what we've done in the Casablanca Stole (shown on page 79). Chevron patterns increase at the highest part of the chevron and decrease at the lowest part of the pattern, giving new life to stripes.

The chart at right shows how the stitches at the top of the chevron pattern, the increase, spread out to create the rounded part of the pattern. The decreases at the bottom of the chevron pattern pull two stitches together to make one stitch. (The chevron pattern is used to elegant effect in The Malibu Breeze Skirt [see page 84].)

74

KEY

Increase—2 sc in 1 st

Decrease—scdec
worked over 2 sts to
create 1 st

Increases and decreases creating chevron pattern

Detail from the Malibu Breeze Skirt on page 84

Bay Blue Hat

This charming hat takes advantage of strategically placed double decreases to create a flirty ruffle that frames your face. A beautiful, lightweight ribbon yarn makes this hat suitable for all seasons.

REFRESH
Crocheting in the round (page 40)
Increases and decreases (page 74)

Finished Size

Circumference: 20" (51 cm)

Ingredients

100 yds (91 m) ¼" (0.6 cm) -wide fine-weight ribbon yarn in blue (MC) **2**

57 yds (52 m) ¼" (0.6 cm) -wide fine-weight ribbon yarn in purple (CC) **2**

Size F/5 (3.75 mm) crochet hook, or size to obtain gauge

Tapestry needle

Stitch markers (optional)

Shown: Berroco Zen (40% cotton, 60% nylon; 110 yds [100.5 m] per 50 g ball):
#8241 Shiseido Blue (MC), 1 ball
#8219 Haiku Purple (CC), 1 ball

Gauge

15 sts = 4" (10 cm) in hdc
11 rows = 4" (10 cm) in hdc
Don't free-pour; do a gauge swatch!

Stitch Explanation

Dc3tog—*yo and insert hook into next st, yo hook and draw up loop, yo and pull through first 2 loops on hook*; rep from * to * 2 more times (there will be 4 loops on hook), yo and pull through all 4 loops on hook.

Make Ruffle

Using CC, ch 252. Sl st in first ch to form ring, being careful not to twist.
Rnd 1: Ch 2, hdc in each ch around. Sl st in top of ch-2 to join. Change to MC.
Rnd 2: Ch 3, dc in next hdc, dc3tog, *dc in next 4 hdc, dc3tog*; rep from * to * around, end dc in next 2 hdc. Sl st in top of ch-3 to join—179 sts rem. Change to CC.
Rnd 3: Ch 3, dc3tog, *dc in next 2 dc, dc3tog*; rep from * to * around, end dc in last dc. Sl st in top of ch-3 to join—107 sts rem. Change to MC.
Rnd 4: Ch 2, dcdec, then dc3tog around. Sl st in top of ch-2 space—36 sts rem. Change to CC.

77

Make Crown

Rnd 5: Ch 1, 2 sc in each st around. Sl st in first sc to join—72 scs rem.

Rnds 6–7: Ch 1, sl st in each st around. Sl st in top of ch-1 to join. Change to MC.

Rnd 8: Ch 2, hdc in back of each sl st around, so that previous row pops out. Sl st in top of ch-2 to join.

Rnds 9–10: Ch 2, hdc in each st around. Sl st in top of ch-2 to join. Change to CC.

Rnds 11–12: Ch 1, sl st in each st around. Sl st in top of ch-1 to join.

Rnd 13: Ch 2, hdc in back of each sl st around, so that previous row pops out. Sl st in top of ch-2 to join. Change to MC.

Rnd 14: Ch 2, hdc in each st around. Sl st in top of ch-2 to join.

Rnd 15: Ch 1, *sc in next 4 sts, scdec*; rep from * to * around, sl st in first sc to join—60 scs rem.

Rnds 16–17: Ch 2, hdc in each st around. Sl st in top of ch-2 to join.

Rnd 18: Ch 1, *sc in next 3 sts, scdec*; rep from * to * around, sl st in first sc to join—48 scs rem.

Rnd 19: Ch 2, hdc in each st around. Sl st in top of ch-2 to join.

Rnd 20: Ch 1, *sc in next 2 sts, scdec*; rep from * to * around, sl st in first sc to join—36 scs rem.

Rnd 21: Ch 2, hdc in each st around. Sl st in top of ch-2 to join.

Rnd 22: Ch 1, *sc in next st, scdec*; rep from * to * around, sl st in first sc to join—24 scs rem.

Rnd 23: Ch 2, hdc in each st around. Sl st in top of ch-2 to join.

Rnd 24: Ch 1, scdec around, sl st in first scdec to join—12 scs rem.

Rnd 25: Ch 1, scdec around, sl st in first scdec to join—6 scs rem.

Rnd 26: Ch 1, scdec around, sl st in first scdec to join—3 scs rem.

Cut yarn, leaving a 6" (15 cm) tail. Thread needle with tail and insert through remaining sts. Pull to tighten. Weave in ends.

Tips

- When changing colors for the stripes, make sure to carry yarns loosely up the back of the work. Carrying the yarns up too tightly will cause the fabric to pucker and distort.

- When working on the first row of the ruffle, use stitch markers to mark ch every 20 sts or so. This will make it easier to keep track of your stitch count.

Casablanca Stole

*E*njoy a refreshing new take on crocheted lace. Use lacy net stitch on the outer edges, then decrease in the middle to form the miter, or angle, until all the stitches are gone. Crochet into the edge to form the next square; no seaming needed! Two breathtaking hand-dyed yarns make this stole a work of art, and you, a wrap artist!

REFRESH
Decreases (page 74)

Finished Size

18" (45.5 cm) wide × 63" (160 cm) long

Ingredients

735 yds (672 m) super fine–weight rayon yarn in multicolor browns/greens (MC)

590 yds (540 m) super fine–weight rayon yarn in multicolor purples/coppers (CC)

Size E/4 (3.5 mm) crochet hook, or size to obtain gauge

Tapestry needle

Shown: Blue Heron Yarns Softwist Rayon (100% rayon; 590 yds [540 m] per 264 g ball): Kelp (MC), 2 balls; Water Hyacinth (CC), 1 ball

Gauge

26 sts = 4" (10 cm) in sc

26 rows = 4" (10 cm) in sc

1 square = 3" (7.5 cm) × 3" (7.5 cm)

Don't free-pour; do a gauge swatch!

Stitch Explanation

Sc3tog—(insert hook into next st, yo, draw up loop) three times, yo and draw through all 4 loops on hook. You will have 2 fewer stitches than you did originally.

Dc3tog—*yo and insert hook into next st, yo hook and draw up loop, yo and pull through first 2 loops on hook*; rep from * to * 2 more times (there will be 4 loops on hook), yo and pull through all 4 loops on hook.

First Row of Five Squares

Square 1

With MC, ch 28. Sc in second ch from hook and each ch across—27 scs rem. Ch 4, turn.

Row 1: Skip first 2 sts, *dc in next st, ch 1, skip next st*; rep from * to * four times more, dc3tog, ch 1, rep from * to * five times more, end dc in last st—25 sts rem. Ch 1, turn.

Row 2: Sc in first st, *sc in ch, sc in dc*; rep from * to * four times more, sc3tog, rep from * to * five times more, end sc in top 2 chs of ch-4—23 sts rem. Ch 4, turn.

Row 3: Skip first 2 sts, *dc in next st, ch 1, skip next st*; rep from * to * three times more, dc3tog, ch 1, rep from * to * four times more, end dc in last st—21 sts rem. Ch 1, turn.

Row 4: Sc in first st, *sc in ch, sc in dc*; rep from * to * three times more, sc3tog, rep from * to * four times more, end sc in next 2 chs of ch 4—19 sts rem. Ch 1, turn.

Row 5: Sc in next 8 sts, sc3tog, sc in next 8 sts—7 sts rem. Ch 1, turn.

Row 6: Sc in next 7 sts, sc3tog, sc in next 7 sts—15 sts rem. Ch 1, turn.

Row 7: Sc in next 6 sts, sc3tog, sc in next 6 sts—13 sts rem. Ch 1, turn.

Row 8: Sc in next 5 sts, sc3tog, sc in next 5 sts—11 sts rem. Ch 1, turn.

Row 9: Sc in next 4 sts, sc3tog, sc in next 4 sts—9 sts rem. Ch 1, turn.

Row 10: Sc in next 3 sts, sc3tog, sc in next 3 sts—7 sts rem. Ch 1, turn.

Row 11: Sc in next 2 sts, sc3tog, sc in next 2 sts—5 sts rem. Ch 1, turn.

Row 12: Sc in next st, sc3tog, sc in next st—3 sts rem. Ch 1, turn.

Row 13: Sc3tog, leaving last loop on hook.

Square 2

Attach CC, ch 1 turn. Pick up and sc 13 sts into side of square 1 on previous row, sc into corner st, ch 14, turn. Sc into second ch from hook and each ch across; sc into 14 sts picked up on side of square on previous row—27 scs rem.

Work rows 1–13 of square 1.

Squares 3–5

Rep as for square 2, alternating squares of MC with squares of CC in a checkerboard pattern. At the end of square 5, fasten off.

Second Row of Squares

Note: Continue to alternate squares of MC and CC in a checkerboard pattern.

Square 6

Attach CC. Ch 1, turn. Pick up and sc 13 sts into side of square 1 from previous row, sc into corner st, ch 14, turn. Sc into second ch from hook and next 12 ch; sc into 14 scs picked up from square 1—27 scs rem.

Work rows 1–13 of square 1.

SCHEMATIC AND PLACEMENT OF SQUARES

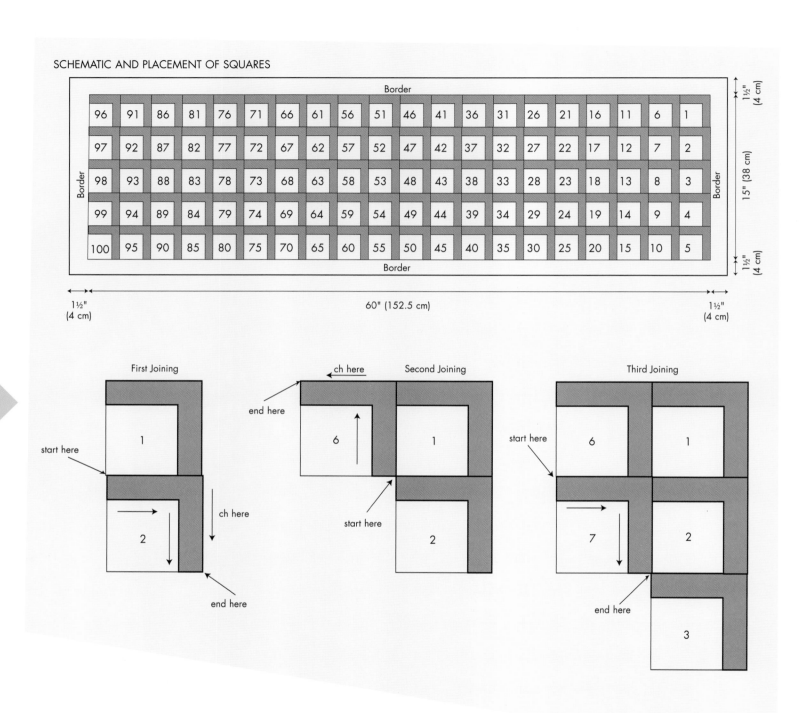

Square 7

Attach MC. Ch 1, turn. Pick up and sc 13 sts along top edge from right to left, sc into corner st, sc into 13 sts along right edge of square 2 of previous row. Ch 1, turn. Sc into each sc across—27 scs rem.

Work rows 1–13 of square 1.

Squares 8–10

Rep as for square 7, alternating squares of MC with squares of CC in a checkerboard pattern. At the end of square 10, fasten off.

Rep second row of squares 18 times more (20 rows of squares, 100 squares total). Fasten off.

Border (worked in rounds)

Rnd 1: Attach MC at one corner. Ch 1, *3 sc into corner st, sc in each st across to next corner*; rep from * to * around, sl st in first sc to join.

Rnd 2: Ch 3, *3 dc into corner st, dc into edge, skipping every fourth st, across to next corner*; rep from * to * around, sl st in top of ch-3.

Rnds 3–4: Ch 3, *3 dc into corner sts, dc in each st across to corner*; rep from * to * around, sl st in top of ch-3. Fasten off. Weave in all ends.

Tip

To maintain sanity, weave in your ends as you go.

Malibu Bay Breeze Skirt

*C*arry the tranquil breezes and the relaxed, free feeling of summer into the colder months with this casual design. Increases and decreases create the shape of this skirt, and they also work together with various colors and textures to create a chevron pattern. Faux pompons in a textured yarn spice up the look.

REFRESH
Loops of a stitch
(page 22)
Crocheting in the round
(page 40)
Popcorn (page 58)
Increases and decreases (page 74)

Finished Size

Small (Medium, Large, XLarge)
25 (30, 35, 40)" [63.5 (76, 89, 101.5) cm] waist circumference
Size shown: Small—25" (63.5 cm)

Ingredients

275 (330, 330, 385) yds [252 (302, 302, 352) m] medium-weight wool yarn in brown (MC) 4

55 yds (50 m) medium-weight wool yarn in green (A) 4

55 yds (50 m) medium-weight wool yarn in fuchsia (B) 4

55 yds (50 m) medium-weight wool yarn in ivory (C) 4

66 yds (60 m) bulky-weight novelty yarn in browns and ivory (D) 5

Size I/9 (5.5 mm) crochet hook, or size to obtain gauge

Size J/10 (6 mm) crochet hook, or size to obtain gauge

3 stitch markers

Tapestry needle

Shown: Tahki Stacy Charles Soho Tweed (100% pure new wool; 110 yds [101 m] per 100 g ball): #354 brown (MC), 5 (6, 6, 7) balls; #333 green (A), #355 fuchsia (B), #301 ivory (C), 1 ball of each; Tahki Stacy Charles Fiorello (100% polyamid; 66 yds [60 m] per 50 g ball): #19 brown/pink/gray (D), 1 ball

Gauge

14½ sc = 4" (10 cm) with MC and smaller hook
12 sc rnds = 4" (10 cm)
12 sts = 4" (10 cm) in chevron pattern with larger hook and yarns as listed
Don't free-pour; do a gauge swatch!

Stitch Explanation

6trpc—work 6 tr into st, remove hook from last loop, insert hook into top of first tr and pull last loop through to secure.

84

Body of Skirt (worked from waist down)

With MC and smaller hook, ch 91 (109, 127, 145), being careful not to twist chs, join with sl st into 1st ch. Pm for beg of rnd.

Rnd 1: Ch 1, sc in each ch around, join into beg ch 1—90 (108, 126, 144) sc rem.

Rnd 2: Ch 1; working in back loop only sc in each sc around, join.

Rnd 3: Ch 2, hdc in both loops in each sc around, join.

Tips

- Use two markers of the same color to indicate the left and right sides of this skirt. It helps to use a different color marker for the beginning of the round.

- The marker for the beginning of the round will shift to one side as each round is worked because of the increased stitches. Use a separate marker for the right side of the garment—if there were only one marker, your increases for the right side would migrate.

- The increases at each side of a garment can be within 2 or 3 stitches of your side marker.

Rnd 4 (Eyelet Rnd): Ch 3, skip hdc, hdc in next hdc, (ch 1, skip hdc, hdc in next hdc) around, ch 1, join into 2nd ch of beg ch 3.

Rnd 5: Ch 2, hdc in each st around, join into ch 2.

Rnd 6: Ch 1, sc in each st around, join into ch 1.

Rnd 7: Working into back loop only, ch 1, 2 sc in first sc for right side of skirt, pm for right side of skirt, sc around, join—91 (109, 127, 145) sts rem.

Rnd 8: Working into both loops, ch 1, 45 (54, 63, 72) sc, pm for left side of skirt, 2 sc in next sc, 45 (54, 63, 72) sc, join—92 (110, 128, 146) sts rem.

For Size Small Only:

Rnds 9–34: Continue increasing as in rnds 7 and 8, working in both loops and increasing one st at each row alternating right and left sides of skirt—118 sts rem.

Rnd 35: Rep rnd 7—119 sts rem.

Rnd 36: Ch 1, sc around.

Rnd 37: Ch 1, sc to marker for left side, 2 sc in next sc, sc around, join—120 sts rem.

Rnd 38: Ch 1, sc around.

Rnd 39: Rep rnd 7—121 sts rem.

Rnds 40–47: Rep rnds 36–39, working increases alternating left and right sides of skirt—125 sts rem.

Rnds 48 and 49: Rep rnds 36 and 37—126 sts rem.

For Size Medium Only:

Rnds 9–32: Continue increasing as in rnds 7 and 8, working in both loops and increasing one st at each row alternating right and left sides of skirt—134 sts rem.

Rnd 33: Rep rnd 7—135 sts rem.

Rnd 34: Ch 1, sc around.

Rnd 35: Ch 1, sc to marker for left side, 2 sc in next sc, sc around, join—136 sts rem.

Rnd 36: Ch 1, sc around.

Rnd 37: Rep rnd 7—137 sts rem.

Rnds 38–49: Rep rnds 34–37—143 sts rem

Rnds 50 and 51: Rep rnds 34 and 35—144 sts rem.

For Size Large Only:

Rnds 9–30: Continue increasing as in rnds 7 and 8, working in both loops and increasing one st at each row alternating right and left sides of skirt—150 sts rem.

Rnd 31: Ch 1, sc around.

Rnd 32: Rep rnd 7—151 sts rem.

Rnd 33: Ch 1, sc around.

Rnd 34: Ch 1, sc to marker for left side, 2 sc in next sc, sc around, join—152 sts rem.

Rnds 35–54: Rep rnds 31–34—162 sts rem.

For Size XLarge Only:

Rnds 9–26: Continue increasing as in rnds 7 and 8, working in both loops and increasing one st at each row alternating right and left sides of skirt—164 sts rem.

Rnd 27: Rep rnd 7—165 sts rem.

Rnd 28: Ch 1, sc around.

Rnd 29: Ch 1, sc to marker for left side, 2 sc in next sc, sc around, join—166 sts rem.

Rnd 30: Ch 1, sc around.

Rnd 31: Rep rnd 7—167 sts rem.

Rnds 32–55: Rep rnds 28–31—179 sts rem.

Rnds 56 and 57: Rep rnds 28 and 29—180 sts.

Chevron Pattern—all sizes

(see chevron chart, page 75)

Rnd 1: Continuing with MC, change to larger hook, ch 2, *2 dc, 2 hdc, 6 sc, 2 hdc, 2 dc, 4 tr*; rep from * to * 6 (7, 8, 9) times more, sl st into top of beg dc to join.

Rnd 2: Ch 1, sc into same st as joining, 4 sc, *(scdec) twice, 6 sc, 2 sc in each of next 2 sc, 6 sc*; rep from * to * 5 (6, 7, 8) times more, (scdec) twice, 6 sc, 2 sc in each of next 2 sc, sc, sl st in first sc to join.

Rnd 3: Change to C, ch 1, sc into same sc as joining, 3 sc, *(scdec) twice, 6 sc, 2 sc in each of next 2 sc, 6 sc*; rep from * to * 5 (6, 7, 8) times more, (scdec) twice, 6 sc, 2 sc in each of next 2 sc, 2 sc, sl st into first sc to join.

Rnd 4: Change to B, ch 1, sc in same sc as joining, 2 sc, *(scdec) twice, 6 sc, 2 sc in each of next 2 sc, 6 sc*; rep from * to * 5 (6, 7, 8) times more, (scdec) twice, 6 sc, 2 sc in each of next 2 sc, 3 sc, sl st into first sc to join.

Rnd 5: Change to A, ch 1, sc in same sc as joining, 1 sc, *(scdec) twice, 6 sc, 2 sc in each of next 2 sc, 6 sc*; rep from * to * 5 (6, 7, 8) times more, (scdec) twice, 6 sc, 2 sc in each of next 2 sc, 4 sc, sl st into first sc to join.

Rnd 6: Change to D, ch 1, turn work so that WS faces you, sc in each st around, sl st into 1st sc to join.

Rnds 7 and 8: Change to A, turn work so that RS faces you, rep rnd 5.

Rnds 9 and 10: Change to B, rep rnd 5.

Rnd 11: Change to D, turn work so that WS faces you, ch 1, sc in each st around, sl st into 1st sc to join.

Fasten off. Weave in ends.

Drawstring

With B, ch a length that measures 35 (40, 45, 50)" [89 (101.5, 114.5, 127) cm]. Weave this length in and out of rnd 4 (eyelet rnd). Tie into a bow. With D, work 6trpc into the beg ch at one end. Fasten off. Knot the beginning and ending yarn tails and weave them into pc. Make another pc at the other end of ch. Fasten off. Weave in ends.

SCHEMATIC

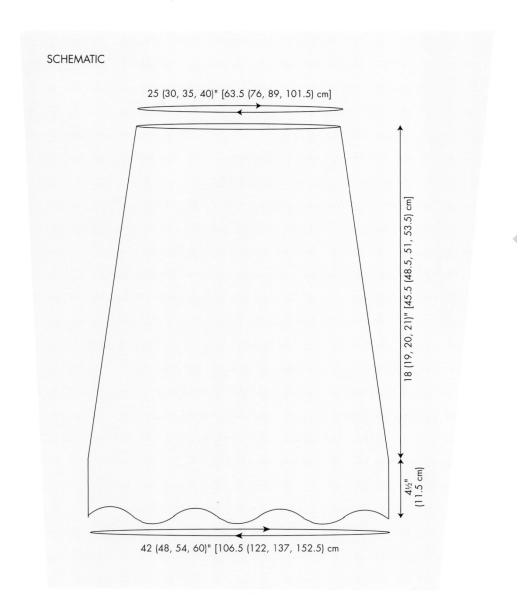

25 (30, 35, 40)" [63.5 (76, 89, 101.5) cm]

18 (19, 20, 21)" [45.5 (48.5, 51, 53.5) cm]

4½" (11.5 cm)

42 (48, 54, 60)" [106.5 (122, 137, 152.5) cm

87

Ocean View Corset

*W*hat a fair maiden you will be, when you adorn yourself in this Renaissance-inspired corset! A sumptuous alpaca yarn wraps your torso in luxury; its subtle touch of glitz accents the undulating wave pattern. Lace up the front with a golden ribbon, and spend an evening at home with your knight in shining armor!

REFRESH
Increases and decreases (page 74)

Finished Size

Small (Medium, Large, XLarge)—32 (36, 40, 44)" [81.5 (91.5, 101.5, 112) cm] chest circumference

Actual chest size of garment (not including lacing): 29½ (34, 37, 41½)" [75 (86.5, 95, 105.5) cm]

Size shown: Small—32" (81.5 cm)

Ingredients

600 (695, 790, 1060) yds [549 (636, 722, 969) m] super fine–weight alpaca yarn in brown

Size C/2 (2.75 mm) crochet hook, or size to obtain gauge

2 yds (2 m), ⁵⁄₁₆" (10 mm) -wide gold ribbon

Tapestry needle

Shown: The Alpaca Yarn Company Glimmer (95% baby alpaca, 5% polyester; approx 183½ yds [167.5 m] per 50 g ball): #2206 Bronze, 4 (4, 5, 6) balls

Gauge

26 sts in pattern = 4" (10 cm)
12 rows in pattern = 4" (10 cm)
Don't free-pour; do a gauge swatch!

Stitch Explanation

Dc3tog—*yo and insert hook into next st, yo hook and draw up loop, yo and pull through first 2 loops on hook*; rep from * to * 2 more times (there will be 4 loops on hook), yo and pull through all 4 loops on hook.

Corset Bodice

Ch 193 (223, 243, 273).

Row 1: Dc into third ch from hook, *3 dc, dc3tog, 3 dc, 3 dc in next ch*; rep from * to * across, ending with 2 dc in last ch—191 (221, 241, 271) sts rem. Ch 2, turn.

Row 2: Dc in same dc at base of ch 2 in first dc, *3 dc, dc3tog, 3 dc, 3 dc in next dc*; rep from * to * across, ending with 2 dc in top of turning ch. Ch 2, turn.

Rep row 2 another 31 (33, 34, 36) times. Fasten off.

Straps (Make 2)

Ch 103 (113, 123, 133).

Row 1: Rep row 1 from corset body—101 (111, 121, 131) sts rem.

Rows 2–6: Rep row 2 from corset body. Fasten off.

Front Edging

With RS facing, beg at bottom right front edge, attach yarn to bottom corner.

For Size Small and XLarge Only (XLarge is in parentheses):

2 sc in the side of each row for 3 rows, ch 5, skip a row, attach loop by sc to top of next row; rep from * to * 5 (6) times more, 2 sc in the side of each of last 3 rows.

For Size Medium and Large Only (Large is in parentheses):

2 sc in the side of each row for 4 (3) rows, ch 5, skip a row, attach loop by sc into top of next row, *2 sc in the side of each row for 3 (5) rows, ch 5, skip a row, attach loop by sc into top of next row*; rep from * to * 4 (3) times, 2 sc in the side of each of last 4 (3) rows.

With RS facing, this time beg at top left front edge, attach yarn to top corner. Rep front edging instructions in appropriate size.

Finishing

Lay corset body on a flat surface. Fold edges of rows in toward the center. Measure the left and right sides to make sure they are equal. Whipstitch the center (about 1" [2.5 cm] from strap side edge) of one end of strap to front about 2¾ (3, 3½, 3½)" [7 (7.5, 9, 9) cm] in from left side fold (shown below). Sew strap to corresponding place at the back of corset bodice. Rep for 2nd strap at right side fold.

Lace the ribbon through the ch-5 loops created by the edging. Begin at the bottom pulling the ribbon through both bottom loops with the tails equal lengths. Cross the lengths and insert into the next loops moving upward along the edging. Continue lacing until you reach the top. Tie a bow.

Weave in ends. Lightly block to smooth out the chevron pattern, if desired.

90

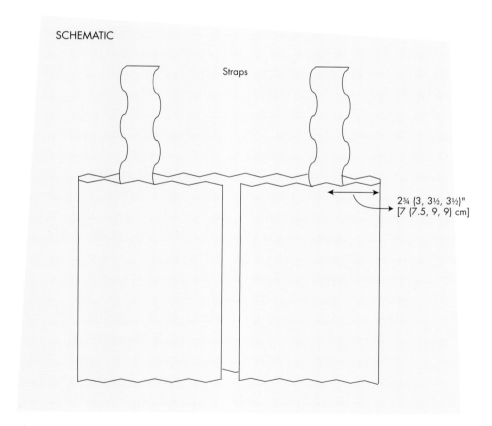

SCHEMATIC

Straps

2¾ (3, 3½, 3½)"
[7 (7.5, 9, 9) cm]

SCHEMATIC

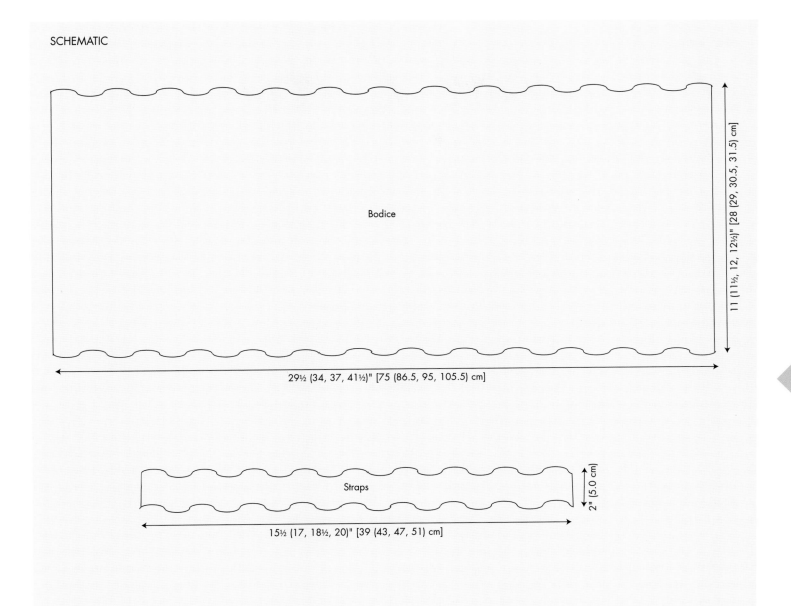

Bodice

11 (11½, 12, 12½)" [28 (29, 30.5, 31.5) cm]

29½ (34, 37, 41½)" [75 (86.5, 95, 105.5) cm]

Straps

2" [5.0 cm]

15½ (17, 18½, 20)" [39 (43, 47, 51) cm]

Martini Drinks

Cable Network

When you think of cables, you most likely think of knitting. But you can also achieve the look of cables with crochet. Remember the Post Stitch in Chapter 1? If you work around the post (see Front Post Double Crochet on page 23) of a stitch in a row below, the new stitch sits on top of the fabric. When these stitches are connected to each other, they create a cabled look. Work the cables on the right side of the fabric. Follow with a row of regular stitches on the wrong side. Repeat these two rows. A chart may help make the cable pattern easier to understand. If you are new to cables, begin with the two patterns that do not have charts and

get used to reading the language. Then, when you're comfortable, test yourself with a pattern that has the rows written out and includes a chart. Finally, challenge yourself with the Bentley Martini Men's Vest (page 107), which relies heavily on the chart. As you gain confidence with reading charts, cabled projects won't seem as daunting.

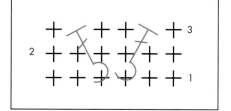

KEY

╋   Sc

Ŧ   FPdc

The charts (shown on this page and opposite) are read from the bottom up. Odd-numbered rows are read from right to left. Even-numbered rows are read from left to right. In the chart on this page, you single crochet across each stitch for the even-numbered row. The action happens on the right side, or odd-numbered rows. That is, the cables are created while working the odd-numbered rows. When you come to an FPdc (see page 23), you work it at the stitch indicated by the hook in the symbol. So, in row 3, you would FPdc around the third sc in row 1. This will create a diagonal line that slants to the right on top of the fabric. Then, sc into the next 2 sc. Work another FPdc but around the post of the fourth sc in row 1. This will create a diagonal line that slants to the left. Then, sc in the last sc.

On the FPdc rows, do not work into the sc behind the FPdc. Skip the sc as listed in the pattern. Remember, the FPdc is the stitch, not the sc. It will increase stitches if you work into the sc behind the FPdc.

When connecting the stitches to form a crossover, work the FPdc in the FPdc on the left in the row below. Then, crochet any stitches in between, if the pattern calls for them. Now the cable cross takes place. FPdc around the FPdc on the right in the row below. It will feel awkward at first, but practice will make perfecto.

Check out the chart on this page showing the crossover happening at row 5. You would work 2 single crochets, skip the first 2 FPdc in row 3, and work a FPdc in the third and fourth FPdc. To finish the crossover, FPdc in the first and second skipped FPdc in row 3. Skip the 4 sc behind the 4 FPdc just worked and single crochet in the last 2 stitches.

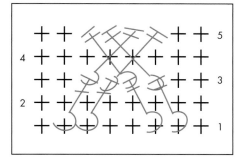

- Work the FPdc a little looser so that this stitch stands out more. It's also easier to complete if worked with a slight looseness.
- After working the front cross cable row, pay special attention to the next sc row to make sure there's a sc in every stitch.

Sweet Vodka Martini Scarf

*U*se this classic scarf to practice the technique of crocheted cables. This scarf has no shaping or complicated patternwork, so you can devote yourself to crossing those post stitches. When it's finished, you will have an elegant scarf for someone special (or keep it yourself!) and you will be well prepared for more complicated cables..

REFRESH
Post stitches (page 23)
Cables (page 92)

Finished Size
6" (15 cm) wide × 68" (172.5 cm) long

Ingredients
308 yds (282 m) bulky-weight alpaca-blend yarn in blue **5**

Size J/10 (6 mm) crochet hook, or size to obtain gauge

Tapestry needle

Shown: The Alpaca Yarn Company Snuggle (55% alpaca, 15% wool, 30% acrylic; 104 yds [95 m] per 100 g ball): #6321 Winter Sky, 3 balls

Gauge
10 sts = 4" (10 cm) in hdc
8 rows = 4" (10 cm) in hdc
Don't free-pour; do a gauge swatch!

Stitch Explanation
Front Cable—skip 2 sts, FPdc under post of next hdc below sc, ch 1, working behind FPdc just made, FPdc under post of hdc of first skipped st.

94

Begin Work

Ch 20.

Row 1 (RS): Hdc in third ch from hook and each ch across—18 hdc rem. Ch 1, turn.

Row 2 and all even rows (WS): Sc in each st across, sc into top of ch-2. Ch 2, turn.

Row 3: Hdc in next 4 scs, *FPdc under post of hdc below next sc, hdc in next sc, FPdc under post of hdc below next sc, hdc in next 4 scs*; rep from * to * once more. Ch 1, turn.

Row 5: Hdc in next 4 scs, *work front cable under posts of hdcs below scs, hdc in next 4 scs*; rep from * to * once more. Ch 1, turn.

Rows 7–9: Rep row 3.

Rep rows 5–9 until scarf measures 67½" (171.5 cm) long or desired length, ending with row 7. Work one row hdc in each st across. Fasten off. Weave in all ends. Wet-block if desired.

Blueberry Martini Bag

Ready for a more complicated cable? This lovely bag uses a cabled strip to form the gusset and strap. Make the front and back in easy single crochet, then challenge yourself with the cable. The cabled strip is crocheted separately, so you don't have to worry about shaping and you can just concentrate on mastering the technique. A crisp linen yarn makes this bag the perfect accent to your summer wardrobe.

REFRESH
Post stitches (page 23)
Cables (page 92)

Finished Size
6" (15 cm) wide × 6" (15 cm) long

Ingredients
300 yds (274.5 m) fine-weight 100% linen yarn **2**

Size B/1 (2.25 mm) crochet hook, or size to obtain gauge

One ¾" (2 cm) button in coordinating color

Tapestry needle

Sewing thread in coordinating color

Shown: Louet North America Euroflax Originals (100% linen; 270 yds [247 m] per 100 g ball): French Blue, 2 balls
¾" (2 cm) polymer clay button (available from Bull's Eye Button—see page 157)

Gauge
22 sts = 4" (10 cm) in sc
28 rows = 4" (10 cm) in sc
Don't free-pour; do a gauge swatch!

Stitch Explanation
FPtr—yo twice, insert hook from front to back around post of st, yo and pull up loop, (yo and pull through 2 loops) 3 times, skip st behind FPtr.

Front Cable—FPtr around fourth and fifth sts from hook, ch 1, FPtr around first two skipped stitches.

96

Back (including flap)

Ch 4, sc in second ch from hook and in each ch across—3 scs rem. Ch 1, turn.

Row 1: 2 sc in next sc, sc across to last st, 2 sc in next sc—5 scs rem. Ch 1, turn.

Row 2: Sc in each sc across.

Rep rows 1 and 2 until you have 35 sts (15 times more). Then rep row 2 until work measures 10" (25.5 cm) from beg. Fasten off.

Front

Ch 36 sts, sc in second ch from hook and each ch across—35 scs. Ch 1, turn.

Row 1: Sc in each sc across.

Rep row 1 until piece measures 6" (15 cm) long. Fasten off.

Cabled Gusset Strap

Row 1: Ch 13 sts, sc in second ch from hook and each ch across—12 scs. Ch 1, turn.

Row 2 and all even-numbered rows: Sc in each st across. Ch 1, turn.

Row 3: Sc in next 2 sts, (FPdc under post of row below in next 2 sc, sc in next st) three times, sc in next st. Ch 1, turn.

Row 5: Sc in next 2 sts, work front cable in next 5 sts, sc in next st, FPdc in next 2 sts, sc in next 2 sts. Ch 1, turn.

Row 7: Sc in next 2 sts, (FPdc in next 2 sts, sc in next st) twice, FPdc in next 2 sts, sc in next 2 sts. Ch 1, turn.

Row 9: Sc in next 2 sts, FPdc in next 2 sts, sc in next st, work front cable over next 5 sts, sc in next 2 sts.

Row 11: Ch 1, turn, sc in next 2 sts, (FPdc in next 2 sts, sc in next st) twice, FPdc in next 2 sts, sc in next 2 sts. Ch 1, turn.

Row 12: Rep row 2.

Rep rows 5–12 twenty-three times more. Fasten off.

Finishing

With RS facing you, sc 30 sts on one side of gusset strap, skipping every fourth sc of gusset edge. Sc gusset strap and back tog, working down one side, across bottom, and then up the other side of back. Continue to sc 30 sts on gusset strap edge only, skipping every fourth sc of gusset edge as before. Fasten off. Rep with other side of gusset strap and front. Join gusset strap ends tog using woven seam method (page 156).

Make button loop: With RS facing you, sc into one edge of flap down to center of point, ch 9, sc in to center of point, sc up the other side edge of the flap. Weave in all ends. Sew button on front of bag to align with button loop.

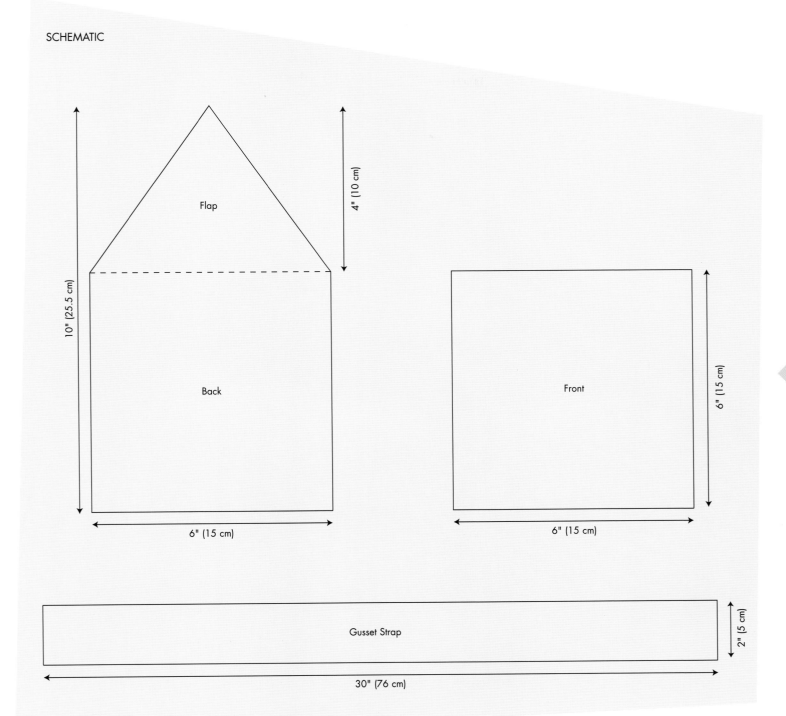

Flap

4" (10 cm)

10" (25.5 cm)

Back

6" (15 cm)

Front

6" (15 cm)

6" (15 cm)

Gusset Strap

2" (5 cm)

30" (76 cm)

Palm Beach Cocktail Purse

*F*un in the sun! This sea- and sand-inspired purse is sure to make waves. Decreases at the edges form its distinctive triangle shape, and front post double crochets make the diamond. A chained loop over the popcorn creates a decorative closure on the back of the purse, while a gold accent sparks up the front of the purse.

REFRESH

Post stitches (page 23)
Loops of a stitch (page 22)
Popcorn (page 58)
Cables (page 92)

Finished Size

8½" (21.5 cm) wide at base, 4½" (11.5 cm) wide at opening × 5½" (14 cm) high, not including handles

Ingredients

250 yds (229 m) medium-weight yarn (4)

Size G/6 (4 mm) crochet hook, or size to obtain gauge

1 Kolláge Yarns Gold Diamond Accentable, about 1¼" (3 cm) long and ¾" (2 cm) wide.

Sewing needle and tan thread

Tapestry needle

Shown: Kolláge Yarns Serenity (merino wool/wool/silk/viscose/polyamide; 100 yds [91 m] per 71 g hank): Sandy Beach, 3 hanks

Gauge

16 sc = 4" (10 cm)
Don't free-pour; do a gauge swatch!

Stitch Explanation

5trpc—work 5 tr, remove hook from loop of last tr, insert it through the top of first tr and into the loop of last tr, pull to gather sts.

Front

Row 1: Ch 36, sc into second ch from hook and into each ch across—35 sc rem. Ch 1, turn.

Rows 2–4: Sc across. Ch 1, turn.

Row 5 (RS): Sc in 2 sc, dc in next sc, sc in next 14 sc, dc in next sc, sc in 14 sc, dc, 2 sc. Ch 1, turn.

Row 6: Sc in each st across. Ch 1, turn.

Row 7: Scdec, sc in next sc, FPdc in dc of row 5 below, skip 1 sc, 11 sc, FPdc in dc of row 5 below, skip 1 sc, 3 sc, FPdc around same dc in row 5, skip 1 sc, 11 sc, FPdc around dc in row 5, skip 1 sc, sc in next sc, scdec—33 sts. Ch 1, turn.

Row 8: Sc across. Ch 1, turn.

Row 9: Scdec, sc in next sc, FPdc around FPdc in row 7, skip 1 sc, sc in next 8 sc, FPdc around FPdc in row 7, skip 1 sc, sc in next 7 sc, FPdc around FPdc in row 7, skip 1 sc, sc in next 8 sc, FPdc around FPdc in row 7, skip 1 sc, sc in next sc, scdec—31 sts. Ch 1, turn.

Row 10: Sc across. Ch 1, turn.

Row 11: Scdec, sc in next sc, FPdc around FPdc in row 9, skip 1 sc, sc in next 6 sc, FPdc around FPdc in row 9, skip 1 sc, sc in next 9 sc, FPdc around FPdc in row 9, skip 1

sc, sc in next 6 sc, FPdc around FPdc in row 9, skip 1 sc, sc in next sc, scdec—29 sts. Ch 1, turn.

Row 12: Sc across. Ch 1, turn.

Row 13: Scdec, sc in next sc, FPdc around FPdc in row 11, skip 1 sc, sc in next 6 sc, FPdc around FPdc in row 11, skip 1 sc, sc in next 7 sc, FPdc around FPdc in row 11, skip 1 sc, sc in next 6 sc, FPdc around FPdc in row 11, skip 1 sc, sc in next sc, scdec—27 sts. Ch 1, turn.

Row 14: Sc across. Ch 1, turn.

Row 15: Scdec, sc in next sc, FPdc around FPdc in row 13, skip 1 sc, sc in next 6 sc, FPdc around FPdc in row 13, skip 1 sc, sc in next 5 sc, FPdc around FPdc in row 13, skip 1 sc, sc in next 6 sc, FPdc around FPdc in row 13, skip 1 sc, sc in next sc, scdec—25 sts. Ch 1, turn.

Row 16: Sc across. Ch 1, turn.

Row 17: Scdec, sc in next sc, FPdc around FPdc in row 15, skip 1 sc, sc in next 6 sc, FPdc around FPdc in row 15, skip 1 sc, sc in next 3 sc, FPdc around FPdc in row 15, skip 1 sc, sc in next 6 sc, FPdc around FPdc in row 15, skip 1 sc, sc in next sc, scdec—23 sts. Ch 1, turn.

Row 18: Sc across. Ch 1, turn.

Row 19: Scdec, sc in next sc, FPdc around FPdc in row 17, skip 1 sc, sc in next 6 sc, FPdc around FPdc in row 17, skip 1 sc, sc in next sc, FPdc around FPdc in row 17, skip 1 sc, sc in next 6 sc, FPdc around FPdc in row 17, skip 1 sc, sc in next sc, scdec—21 sts. Ch 1, turn.

Row 20: Sc across. Ch 1, turn.

Row 21: Scdec, sc in next sc, FPdc around FPdc in row 19, skip 1 sc, sc in next 6 sc, FPdc around right FPdc in row 19 and around left FPdc in row 19, skip 1 sc, sc in next 6 sc, FPdc around FPdc in row 19, sc in next sc, scdec—19 sts. Ch 1, turn.

Rows 22–24: Sc across. Ch 1, turn.

Row 25: Sc in 9 sc, sl st into next sc, ch 30, sl st into same sc, sc in 9 sc—18 sts. Fasten off.

Back

Work as for front, except substitute these instructions for rows 11 and 25:

Row 11: Scdec, sc in next sc, FPdc around FPdc in row 9, skip 1 sc, sc in next 6 sc, FPdc around FPdc in row 9, skip 1 sc, sc in next 4 sc, 5trpc in next st, sc in next 4 sc, FPdc around FPdc in row 9, skip 1 sc, sc in next 6 sc, FPdc around FPdc in

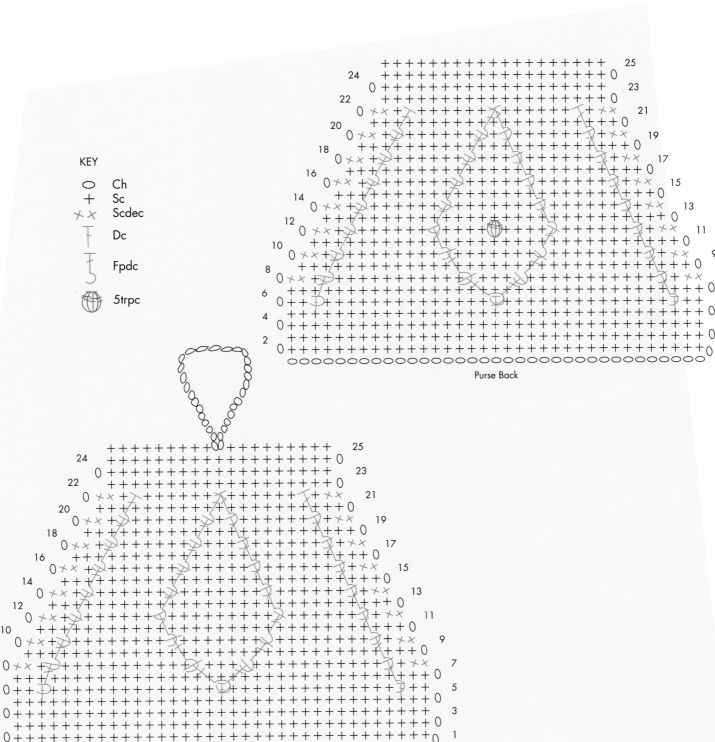

KEY

⬭ Ch	
+ Sc	
×× Scdec	
⊤ Dc	
⌶ Fpdc	
🌐 5trpc	

Purse Back

Purse Front

row 9, skip 1 sc, sc in next sc, scdec—29 sts. Ch 1, turn.

Row 25: Sc across. Fasten off.

Sides and Base

Row 1: Ch 6, sc in second ch from hook and in each ch—5 sc rem. Ch 1, turn.

Rows 2–26: Sc across. Ch 1, turn.

Row 27 (RS): Sc into back loop only. Ch 1, turn.

Rows 28–74: Sc in each sc. Ch 1, turn.

Row 75: Sc into back loop only. Ch 1, turn.

Rows 76–101: Sc across. Do not fasten off. Ch 1, position strip alongside the back of purse (WS tog) and sc the 2 pieces tog, making sure row 27 of the sides and base piece lines

up at the bottom corner. Work 3 sc in same st at corner. Sc the two pieces tog across the bottom of purse. Work 3 sc in same st at corner. Continue sc the two pieces tog to top of purse. Fasten off. Turn purse over so front is facing, attach yarn, and sc the front piece to the sides in same manner. Weave in ends.

Handle (Make 2)

Row 1: Ch 4, sc into second ch from hook and in next 2 chs—3 sc rem. Ch 1, turn.

Rows 2 and 3: Sc across. Ch 1, turn.

Row 4: 2 sc in 1st sc, sc in next sc, 2 sc in last sc—5 sc rem. Ch 1, turn.

Rows 5–45: Sc across. Ch 1, turn.

Row 46: Scdec, sc in next sc, scdec—3 sc rem. Ch 1, turn.

Rows 47 and 48: Sc across. Ch 1, turn.

Row 49: Sc across. Fasten off.

Finishing

Fold one handle in half lengthwise, matching first and last sts of each row. Beg at row 4, insert hook through both layers and sl st them tog. Continue sl st the first and last sts tog of each row to row 46. Fasten off.

Sew beg and ending flat ends of one handle to inside front of purse. Rep for back with second handle. Using one of the component yarns or sewing thread, attach the diamond accent to the center of the cabled diamond on front of purse. To keep the accent flat, insert one end of the yarn into the hole at the top of the accent and tie a knot. Then, insert the ends of the yarn through the purse fabric through two different sts. Tie the ends into a knot on the WS of purse fabric. Weave in ends.

Tips

- You can pin the pieces to keep them in place during assembly.
- The sides and base of the purse may be made wider by working more beg chains.

104

Bentley Martini Men's Vest

Your favorite man will be shaken and stirred when you serve up this debonair vest. The cable panel is challenging but manageable. Give it a try! Every other row, you get a break from the cable pattern and just cruise along single crocheting. The sweater isn't as heavy as you might think since it's worked in a wonderfully lightweight cotton/acrylic–blend yarn.

REFRESH
Post stitches (page 23)
Cables (page 92)

Finished Size
Small (Medium, Large, XLarge, XXLarge)—36 (38, 40, 42, 44)" [91.5 (96.5, 101.5, 106.5, 112) cm] chest circumference
Size shown: Medium—38" (96.5 cm)

Ingredients
1165 (1248, 1331, 1414, 1497) yds [1065 (1141, 1217, 1293, 1369) m] light-weight cotton/acrylic–blend yarn in light gray (MC) (3)

371 (433, 495, 557, 619) yds [339 (396, 452.5, 509, 566) m] light-weight cotton/acrylic–blend yarn in dark gray (CC) (3)

Size F/5 (3.75 mm) crochet hook

Size G/6 (4 mm) crochet hook, or size to obtain gauge

4 stitch markers

Tapestry needle

Shown: Kraemer Yarns Tatamy Tweed (45% cotton, 55% acrylic; 250 yds [229 m] per 100 g ball): Silver (MC), 5 (5, 6, 6, 7) balls; Flannel Tweed (CC), 2 (2, 3, 3, 3) balls

Gauge
4½ sts = 1" (2.5 cm) in sc on size G/6 (4 mm) hook

5½ rows = 1" (2.5 cm) in sc
Don't free-pour; do a gauge swatch!

Stitch Explanation
BPdc2tog—yo hook, *bring hook around post of st as if working a BPdc, yo hook and pull up loop, yo hook and draw through 2 loops on hook*; yo hook and rep from * to * in next dc, yo hook and pull through all 3 loops on hook.
FPdc2tog—yo hook, *insert hook around post of st as if working a FPdc, yo hook and pull up loop, yo hook and draw through 2 loops on hook*; yo hook and rep from * to * in next dc, yo hook and pull through all 3 loops on hook.

107

Notes:

1: Ch 3 turning chain counts as first st of a row.

2: For sizes Small and Medium, the cable panel width is 16 sts. For sizes Large, XLarge, and XXLarge, the cable panel is 18 sts wide.

Front Ribbing

Row 1: With CC and smaller hook, ch 93 (97, 101, 105, 109), dc into third ch from hook and in each ch across—92 (96, 100, 104, 108) dc. Ch 3, turn.

Row 2 (WS): FPdc around second dc, (BPdc) twice, *(FPdc) twice, (BPdc) twice*; rep from * to * across. Ch 3, turn.

Rows 3–8: Rep row 2. End row 8 with Ch 1, turn.

Body

Row 1 (RS): Change to MC and larger hook, sc across. Ch 1, turn.

Row 2: Sc across. Ch 1, turn.

Cable Panel Setup

For Size Small Only:

Row 3: 14 sc, pm, work 16 sts of chart row 13, pm, 32 sc, pm, rep 16 sts of chart row 13, pm, 14 sc. Ch 1, turn.

Rows 4–12 (Even Rows Only): Sc across. Ch 1, turn.

Rows 5–11 (Odd Rows Only): 14 sc, pm, work next odd row of chart, pm, 32 sc, pm, rep same chart row, pm, 14 sc.

For Size Medium Only:

Row 3: 15 sc, pm, work 16 sts of chart row 11, pm, 34 sc, pm, rep 16 sts of chart row 11, pm, 15 sc. Ch 1, turn.

Rows 4–14 (Even Rows Only): Sc across. Ch 1, turn.

Rows 5–13 (Odd Rows Only): 15 sc, pm, work next odd row of chart, pm, 34 sc, pm, rep same chart row, pm, 15 sc. Ch 1, turn.

For Size Large Only:

Row 3: 15 sc, pm, work 18 sts of chart row 9, pm, 34 sc, pm, rep 18 sts of chart row 9 of chart, pm, 15 sc. Ch 1, turn.

Rows 4–16 (Even Rows Only): Sc across. Ch 1, turn.

Rows 5–15 (Odd Rows Only): 15 sc, pm, work next odd row of chart, pm, 34 sc, pm, rep same chart row, pm, 15 sc. Ch 1, turn.

For Size XLarge Only:

Row 3: 16 sc, pm, work 18 sts of chart row 5, pm, 36 sc, pm, rep 18 sts of chart row 5, pm, 16 sc. Ch 1, turn.

Rows 4–20 (Even Rows Only): Sc across. Ch 1, turn.

Rows 5–19 (Odd Rows Only): 16 sc, pm, work next odd row of chart, pm, 36 sc, pm, rep same chart row, pm, 16 sc. Ch 1, turn.

Size XXLarge Only:

Row 3: 17 sc, pm, 1 sc, work 18 sts of chart row 1 of chart, pm, 36 sc, pm, rep 18 sts of chart row 1, 1 sc, pm, 17 sc. Ch 1, turn.

Rows 4–22 (Even Rows Only): Sc across. Ch 1, turn.

Rows 5–21 (Odd Rows Only): 17 sc, pm, 1 sc, work next odd row of chart, pm, 36 sc, pm, rep same chart row, 1 sc, pm, 17 sc. Ch 1, turn.

Full Cable—all sizes

Work even in established pattern, continuing to work cable panel repeat frame from chart.

Armholes

When piece measures 15 (15, 15½, 16, 16)" [38 (38, 39, 40.5, 40.5) cm] from beg, sl st in first 13 (14, 15, 16, 17) sc of next 2 rows—66 (68, 70, 72, 74) sc.

Work even, continuing cable pattern for 4½ (4¾, 4¾, 5, 5¼)" [11.5 (12, 12, 12.5, 13.5) cm] from beg of armhole shaping, ending with a WS row.

Decrease for V-Neck

For Size Small Only:

Left Side of Neck

Row 1 (RS): Continuing the established cable pattern, work 31 sts, scdec—32 sts rem. Ch 1, turn.

Rows 2–22 (Even Rows Only): Sc across. Ch 1, turn.

Rows 3–23 (Odd Rows Only): Keeping in pattern, work to last 2 sts, scdec—-21 sts rem after row 23 is complete. Ch 1, turn.

Rows 24–35: Keeping in pattern, scdec at neck edge every third row 4 times (rows 26, 29, 32, and 35)—17 sts rem after row 35 is complete. Ch 1, turn.

Row 36: Sc across. Fasten off.

Right Side of Neck

Row 1 (RS): With slip knot on hook, scdec beg in the 34th st of row 1, sc across—32 sts.

Rep instructions from left side of neck, reversing the shaping to maintain dec at neck edge.

For Size Medium Only:

Left Side of Neck

Row 1 (RS): Continuing the established cable pattern, work 32 sts, scdec—33 sts rem. Ch 1, turn.

Rows 2–28 (Even Rows Only): Sc across. Ch 1, turn.

Rows 3–27 (Odd Rows Only): Keeping in pattern, work to last 2 sts, scdec—20 sts rem. Ch 1, turn.

Rows 29–36: Ch 1, turn, keeping in pattern, scdec at neck edge every fourth row 2 times (rows 32 and 36)—18 sts rem. Fasten off.

Right Side of Neck

Row 1 (RS): With slip knot on hook, scdec beg in the 35th st of row 1, sc across—33 sts rem.

Rep instructions from left side of neck, reversing the shaping to maintain dec at neck edge.

For Size Large Only:

Left Side of Neck

Row 1 (RS): Continuing the established cable pattern, work 33 sts, scdec—34 sts rem. Ch 1, turn.

Rows 2–26 (Even Rows Only): Sc across. Ch 1, turn.

Rows 3–27 (Odd Rows Only): Keeping in pattern, work to last 2 sts, scdec—21 sts rem. Ch 1, turn.

Rows 28–36: Keeping in pattern, scdec at neck edge every third row 3 times (rows 30, 33, and 36)—18 sts rem. Ch 1, turn.

Row 37: Sc across. Fasten off.

Right Side of Neck

Row 1 (RS): With slip knot on hook, scdec beg in the 36th st of row 1, sc across—34 sts rem. Ch 1, turn.

Rep instructions from left side of neck, reversing the shaping to maintain dec at neck edge.

For Size XLarge Only:

Left Side of Neck

Row 1 (RS): Continuing the established cable pattern, work 34 sts, scdec—35 sts rem. Ch 1, turn.

Rows 2–24 (Even Rows Only): Sc across. Ch 1, turn.

Rows 3–25 (Odd Rows Only): Keeping in pattern, work to last 2 sts, scdec—23 sts. Ch 1, turn.

Rows 26–40: Keeping in pattern, scdec at neck edge every third row 5 times (rows 28, 31, 34, 37, and 40)—18 sts rem.

Row 41: Sc across. Fasten off.

Right Side of Neck

Row 1 (RS): With slip knot on hook, scdec beg in the 37th st of row 1, sc across—35 sts rem. Ch 1, turn.

Rep instructions from left side of neck, reversing the shaping to maintain dec at neck edge.

For Size XXLarge Only:

Left Side of Neck

Row 1 (RS): Continuing the established cable pattern, work 35 sts, scdec—36 sts rem. Ch 1, turn.

Rows 2–20 (Even Rows Only): Sc across. Ch 1, turn.

Rows 3–21 (Odd Rows Only): Keeping in pattern, work to last 2 sts, scdec—26 sts rem. Ch 1, turn.

Rows 22–42: Keeping in pattern, scdec at neck edge every third row 7 times (rows 24, 27, 30, 33, 36, 39, and 42)—19 sts rem. Ch 1, turn.

Row 43: Sc across. Fasten off.

Right Side of Neck

Row 1 (RS): With slip knot on hook, scdec beg in the 38th st of row 1, sc across—36 sts rem. Ch 1, turn.

Rep instructions from left side of neck, reversing the shaping to maintain dec at neck edge.

Back

Rep instructions as for front ribbing.

Body

Row 1 (RS): Change to MC and larger hook, ch 1, turn, sc across. Work even until piece measures 15 (15, 15½, 16, 16)" [38 (38, 39, 40.5, 40.5) cm] from beg, ending with a WS row.

Armholes

Row 1 (RS): Sl st in first 13 (14, 15, 16, 17) sc, pm, work across keeping in pattern.

Row 2: Sl st in first 13 (14, 15, 16, 17) sc, sc across to marker—66 (68, 70, 72, 74) sts.

Keeping in pattern, work even for 11 (11¼, 11¾, 12½, 13¼)" [28 (28.5, 30, 31.5, 33.5) cm] from beg of armhole shaping. Fasten off.

Finishing

Place front and back pieces with RS and armhole edges tog, and sl st them tog at shoulder seams.

Armhole Edging

Left Side

Row 1: With RS facing, CC and smaller hook, attach yarn to front piece and dc across sl sts at armhole, work 3 dcdec at front armhole corner (before, at center, and after the right angle at armhole), dc in edge of each row up front and down back, work 3 dcdec at back armhole corner (before, at center, and after the right angle at armhole), dc across sl sts at armhole. Sts may be added or skipped to make sure the total number of sts in row 1 is divisible by 4. Ch 3, turn.

Row 2: Fpdc around second dc, (BPdc) twice, *(FPdc) twice, (BPdc) twice*; rep from * to * across. Ch 3, turn.

Row 3: FPdc, *(BPdc) twice, (FPdc) twice*; rep from * to * across, working (BPdc2tog, FPdc2tog) at front and back armhole corners.

Right Side

Rep for right side armhole.

Place front and back pieces with RS tog, and use woven seam method (page 156) and CC to sew armhole and bottom edgings. With MC, sl st front and back pieces tog at side seams.

Neck Edging

Row 1: With RS facing, CC and smaller hook, attach yarn to front at bottom of "v", dc in edge of each row and st around neck. Sts may be added or skipped to make sure total sts are divisible by 4. Do not join. Ch 3, turn.

Row 2: FPdc around 2nd dc, (BPdc) twice, *(FPdc) twice, (BPdc) twice*; rep from * to * across. Ch 3, turn.

Row 3: FPdc, *BPdc2tog, FPdc2tog*; rep from * to * across. Fasten off.

Place beg and ending edges of ribbing tog and use woven seam method (page 156) to attach them.

Weave ends into WS.

CABLE PANEL   SCHEMATIC

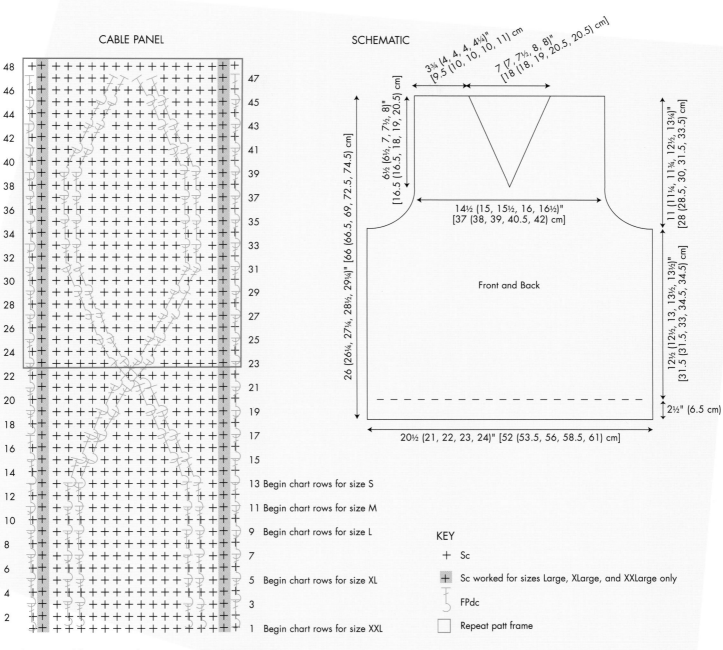

KEY

+   Sc

+   Sc worked for sizes Large, XLarge, and XXLarge only

⌡   FPdc

☐   Repeat patt frame

Work 16-st panel for sizes S and M (omit scs in green background)
Work 18-st panel for sizes L, XL, and XXL (include scs in green background)

Begin chart rows for size S
Begin chart rows for size M
Begin chart rows for size L
Begin chart rows for size XL
Begin chart rows for size XXL

Coffee Drinks

Feelin' Hot, Hot, Hot!

Ah, the magic of felting! Felting is like going to the gym. You start out loose and floppy, and end up firm and fabulous. It takes a little work, but it's all worth it in the end.

What exactly is felting? Felting involves making a fabric out of compressed animal fibers. Crocheters accomplish this by putting a loosely crocheted fabric in a hot water wash, usually with the aid of a washing machine and a little liquid dish soap. The resulting fabric is as tight as you want to make it, and completely unique. The fabric also hides imperfections: uneven gauge or ugly holes get closed up, so you look like a pro.

First of all, choose your yarn. Select 100 percent animal fibers, such as wool, mohair, alpaca, and llama, for best results. If you like to take risks, it is possible to felt some yarns that contain a small amount of plant or synthetic fiber. It is absolutely vital that you make a gauge swatch and run it through the felting process before you begin your project. No, really! Each yarn is going to behave differently when you put it in the hot wash. You may find that a yarn that looks luscious in the skein loses its flavor after taking a hot bath. For example, alpaca felts to a softer fabric with more drape than wool. You might not want to use it for a purse, which needs a firm fabric to withstand everyday wear and tear. Even some 100 percent sheep wools felt differently, depending on the breed of sheep, and superwash wool is specially treated to prevent exactly what you're trying to do. So, make sure that you don't free-pour on this one.

Crochet your gauge swatch. Keep in mind that crocheting to the unfelted gauge does not guarantee that the finished project will felt to the correct dimensions. Take four pieces of synthetic or plant-fiber yarn, and use them to mark off a 4" (10 cm) square in the swatch (top photo, opposite page). We'll use them later to measure how much the square shrank after felting (bottom photo, opposite page), and compare its felted gauge with the felted gauge of the project.

Now, here comes the exciting part. Put your crochet piece in a zippered pillowcase or mesh bag (in case it sheds) and place it in the washing machine with something heavy, like a pair of old jeans, to ensure its agitation. Set the washer for hot and put in a small amount of liquid dish soap. While it's filling up, run and get your kitchen timer. Set the timer for 3 to 5 minutes, to remind you to stop the washer and check to see how your felting is progressing. You are in charge! When the felted crochet looks like it's approaching the correct dimensions, take it out and rinse it with cold water in your sink to firm up the fabric, then gently shape it to your desired dimensions and place on a drying rack to dry.

When you're felting your gauge swatch, you may notice that the middle of the swatch felts faster than the outside edges. This is called "splay." Don't worry, your *Yarn Cocktails* directions are written to compensate for splay. Finally, measure the 4" (10 cm) square you marked off before putting the swatch in the wash. See how much it shrank? This is your felted gauge. Now, you're ready for action!

Unfelted swatch

Felted swatch

Chambord Coffee French Wallet

This French-style wallet will have you saying Ooh, la la! A departure from traditional wallets, this hottie has a pocket for your cash and even a pocket in the back for your credit card or driver's license. Tuck it into your bag and enjoy.

The wallet is made in one piece, then folded and sewn together. An additional pocket is created separately and sewn onto the back for your cards.

 **REFRESH**
Felting (page 112)

Finished Size (after felting)
About 9" (23 cm) × 4¼" (11 cm) after wallet is folded

Ingredients
100 yds (91.5 m) light-weight wool/mohair–blend yarn (see *Note*)

Size H/8 (5 mm) crochet hook, or size to obtain unfelted gauge

Sew-on snap

Sewing needle and thread in coordinating color

Tapestry needle

Note: Don't use superwash wool, or 100% synthetics, because they won't felt. If you choose a blended yarn, it should contain at least 50% or more wool in order to obtain similar felting percentage as the project.

Shown: Mountain Colors Mountain Goat (55% mohair, 45% wool; approx 230 yds [210 m] per 100 g hank): Ruby River, 1 hank

Unfelted Gauge
13 sc = 4" (10 cm) in sc
20 rows = 4" (10 cm) in sc

Felted Gauge
13 sc = 3¼" (8.5 cm) in sc
20 rows = 3¼" (8.5 cm) in sc
Don't free-pour; do a gauge swatch!

Wallet
Ch 33.
Row 1: Sc in second ch from hook and each ch across—32 sc rem. Ch 1, turn.
Rows 2–5: Sc in each sc across. Ch 1, turn.

Row 6: Sc in next 2 sc, *2 sc in next sc, sc in next 8 sc*; rep from * to * twice more, 2 sc in next sc, sc in next 2 sc—36 sc rem. Ch 1, turn.

Rows 7–40: Sc in each sc across. Ch 1, turn.

Row 41: Sc in next 2 sc, *scdec, sc in next 8 sc*; rep from * to * twice more, scdec, sc in next 2 sc—32 sc rem. Ch 1, turn.

Rows 42–46: Sc in each sc across. Ch 1 turn.

Flap

Rows 1–10: Scdec, sc in each sc across to last 2 sts, scdec—12 sts rem. Ch 1, turn. Omit ch 1 at end of row 10 and fasten off.

Driver's License Pocket

Ch 13.

Row 1: Sc in second ch from hook and each ch across—12 sc rem. Ch 1, turn.

Rows 2–15: Sc in each sc across. Ch 1, turn. Omit ch 1 at end of row 15 and fasten off.

Finishing

Fold piece at 23rd row from beg. Starting at fold line on left side, sc sides tog row for row. Continue to sc around front flap only, then sc both sides tog on other side row for row. Center driver's license pocket on back of wallet and whipstitch on 3 sides, leaving top open. Weave in all ends. Felt wallet (see page 112).

Shape and lay flat to dry. Insert card in pocket to stretch and shape it. When dry, sew snap to inside of wallet flap and corresponding location on outside of wallet.

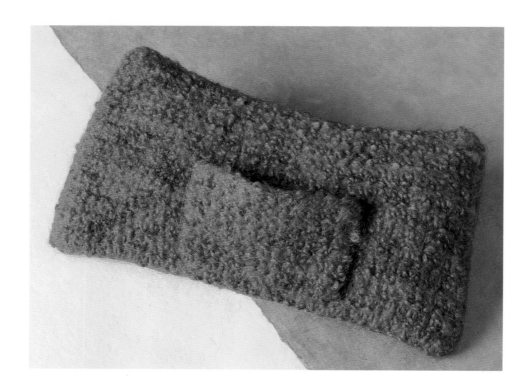

ASSEMBLY INSTRUCTIONS AND SCHEMATIC

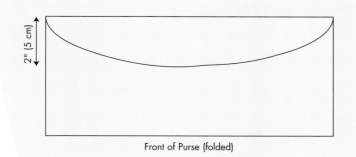

Front of Purse (folded)

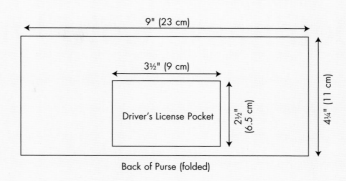

Back of Purse (folded)

Driver's License Pocket

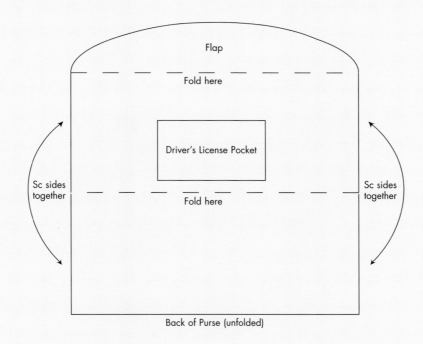

Back of Purse (unfolded)

Caribbean Coffee Demitasse Coin Purse

This coin purse serves as a gauge swatch as well as holding your spare change. Use it to practice felting in your washer before tackling a larger felting project: the backpack. A little taste of things to come: this lively yarn evokes the beauty of a Caribbean sunrise. Wake up and smell the coffee!

REFRESH
Crocheting in the round (page 40)
Felting (page 112)

Finished Size (after felting)
About 4½" (11.5 cm) wide (including edging) × 4" (10 cm) high (not including flap)

Ingredients
75 yds (69 m) medium-weight wool yarn (see *Note*, page 114)

Size K/10½ (6.5 mm) crochet hook, or size to obtain unfelted gauge

One ½" (1.3 cm) glass button

Sewing needle and coordinating thread

Tapestry needle

Shown: South West Trading Company Karaoke (50% wool, 50% soy silk; approx 110 yds [100 m] per 50 g ball): #297 Playful, 1 ball

Unfelted Gauge
11 sts = 4" (10 cm) in sc
14 rows = 4" (10 cm) in sc

Felted Gauge
11 sts = 3" (7.5 cm) in sc
14 rows = 3½" (9 cm) in sc
Don't free-pour; do a gauge swatch!

118

Front of Purse

Ch 3. Sl st in first ch to form ring.

Rnd 1: Ch 1, 6 sc in ring. Sl st in first sc to join.

Rnd 2: Ch 1, 2 sc in each sc around—12 sc. Join.

Rnd 3: Ch 1, *sc in sc, 2 sc in next sc*; rep from * to * around—18 sc. Join.

Rnd 4: Ch 1, *sc in next 2 sc, 2 sc in next sc*; rep from * to * around—24 sc. Join.

Rnd 5: Ch 1, *sc in next 3 sc, 2 sc in next sc*; rep from * to * around—30 sc. Join.

Rnd 6: Ch 1, *sc in next 4 sc, 2 sc in next sc*; rep from * to * around—36 sc. Join.

Rnd 7: Ch 1, *sc in next 5 sc, 2 sc in next sc*; rep from * to * around—42 sc. Join.

Fasten off.

Back of Purse

Make same as for front of purse. Do not fasten off.

With RS facing outward, sc front and back of purse together. Sc around into both pieces for the next 31 sts, then sc into rem 11 sts on back of purse ONLY, leaving top of purse open. Ch 1, turn to face other side.

Flap

Row 1: Working back and forth, sc across 11 sts on back of purse. Ch 1, turn.

Row 2: Scdec, sc to last 2 sts, scdec—9 sts.

Rep Row 2 until 5 sts rem. Fasten off.

Edging

Attach yarn at right edge of circle next to opening. Sl st into first sc joining front and back of purse together, *ch 3, sl st into next sc; rep from * around circle, then down left side of flap. Work (ch 3, sl st into next sc) 3 times at top of flap. Ch 5, sl st back into same sc to form button loop. Work (ch 3, sl st into next sc) 3 times to continue edging at top of flap. Rep from * up right side of flap, sl st into first sc joining front and back of purse. Fasten off. Weave in ends. Felt coin purse (see page 112).

Shape and lay flat to dry. If desired, separate loops of edging. When dry, sew on button opposite button loop.

Caribbean Coffee Grande Convertible Backpack/Purse

*M*ade your coin purse? Then you're ready for this shoulder bag, which converts easily into a backpack by threading the strap through the loops on the back. Tuck the coin purse inside for a matching set, and you're ready to do some island-hopping! Enjoy the long color repeats washing over this convertible backpack like sunrise on the waters of the Caribbean.

This bag consists of two crocheted circles. Three crocheted rectangles are sewn to the back of the bag to form loops. A long crocheted strap is threaded through the top loop and tied to create a shoulder bag, or the strap can be threaded through all three loops and tied to form a backpack.

REFRESH
Crocheting in the round (page 40)
Felting (page 112)

Finished Size (after felting)

11" (28 cm) wide × 9½" (24 cm) high (not including flap)

Ingredients

550 yds (500 m) medium-weight wool yarn (see *Note*, page 114) **4**

Size K/10½ (6.5 mm) crochet hook, or size to obtain unfelted gauge

One ⅞" (2.2 cm) glass button

Sewing needle and coordinating thread

Tapestry needle

Shown: South West Trading Company Karaoke (50% wool, 50% soy silk; about 110 yds [100 m] per 50 g ball): #297 Playful, 1 ball

Unfelted Gauge

11 sts = 4" (10 cm) in sc
14 rows = 4" (10 cm) in sc

Felted Gauge

11 sts = 3" (7.5 cm) in sc
14 rows = 3½" (9 cm) in sc
Don't free-pour; do a gauge swatch!

Front of Backpack

Ch 3. Sl st in first ch to form ring.

Rnd 1: Ch 1, 6 sc in ring. Sl st in first sc to join.

Rnd 2: Ch 1, 2 sc in each sc around—12 sc rem. Join.

Rnd 3: Ch 1, *sc in sc, 2 sc in next sc*; rep from * to * around—18 sc rem. Join.

Rnd 4: Ch 1, *sc in next 2 sc, 2 sc in next sc*; rep from * to * around—24 sc rem. Join.

Rnd 5: Ch 1, *sc in next 3 sc, 2 sc in next sc*; rep from * to * around—30 sc. Join.

Continue as above, increasing 6 sc evenly spaced in each of next 15 rounds until 120 sc rem.

Next 3 rnds: Ch 1, sc in each sc. Join. Fasten off after completing last rnd.

Back of Backpack

Make same as for front of backpack. Do not fasten off.

With RS facing (WS tog), sc front and back of backpack together. Sc around into both pieces for the next 93 sts, then sc into rem 27 sts on back of backpack ONLY, leaving top of backpack open. Ch 1, turn to face other side.

Flap

Row 1: Working back and forth, sc across 27 sts on back of backpack. Ch 1, turn.

Rows 2–4: Rep row 1.

Row 5: Sc, scdec, sc to last 3 sts, scdec, sc—25 sts rem.

Next 7 rows: Repeat row 5 until 11 sts rem. Fasten off.

Edging

Attach yarn at right edge of circle next to opening. Sl st into first sc joining front and back of backpack together, *ch 5, sl sl into next sc; rep from * around circle, then along left side of flap. Work (ch 5, sl st in next sc) 6 times at top of flap. Ch 9, sl st back into same sc to form button loop. Work (ch 5, sl st in next sc) 6 times to continue edging at top of flap. Rep from * along right side of flap, sl st into first sc joining front and back of backpack. Fasten off. Weave in ends.

Large Backpack Loop (Make 1)

Ch 13. Sc in second ch from hook, sc across—12 sts rem. Ch 1, turn.

Sc across until piece is 3½" (9 cm) long. Fasten off.

Small Backpack Loops (Make 2)

Ch 9 sts. Sc in second ch from hook, sc across—8 sts rem. Ch 1, turn.

Sc across until piece is 3½" (9 cm) long. Fasten off.

Strap

Ch 5. Sc in second ch from hook, sc across—4 sts rem. Ch 1, turn.

Rows 1 and 2: Sc across. Ch 1, turn.

Row 3 (Increase Row): Sc in next sc, 2 sc in next sc, sc in next 2 sc—5 sts rem.

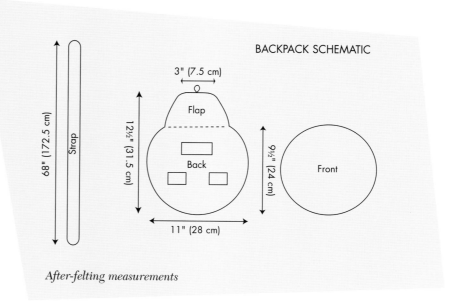

After-felting measurements

BACKPACK SCHEMATIC

3" (7.5 cm)

Flap

Back

Front

68" (172.5 cm) Strap

12½" (31.5 cm)

9½" (24 cm)

11" (28 cm)

Rep row 1 until strap measures 71" (180.5 cm) from beg.

Dec Row: Sc in next sc, scdec, sc in next 2 sc—4 sts rem.

Rep row 1 three times more. Fasten off.

Finishing

Sew top edge of large backpack loop to top center of back of backpack, about 16 rows down from edge of flap. Count down 4 rows and sew lower edge of large backpack loop. Sew top edge of small backpack loop to lower right edge of back of backpack. Count down 4 rows and sew lower edge of small backpack loop. Repeat process with second small backpack loop on lower left edge of back of backpack.

Weave in all ends. Felt purse (see page 112).

Shape and lay flat to dry. When dry, sew on button opposite button loop.

Adjusting Straps

To wear as a shoulder bag, pull strap through large backpack loop and knot at desired length to secure. To wear as a backpack, pull strap through all three loops and knot at desired length to secure.

Baja Coffee Necklace

Perk up your wardrobe with this lively combination of turquoise and coffee flavors. The beads are fun and fast to crochet. Hand-felting allows you to work out any stress as you watch each bead transform into a fanciful felted treasure. Stringing lightweight crochet beads with stone beads brews up this steamy little number.

REFRESH

Crocheting in the round (page 40)

Front loop only (page 22)

Finished Size

22" (56 cm) long

Ingredients

50 yds (45.5 m) medium-weight wool yarn (see *Note*, page 114) 🧶4

10 yds (9 m) nonfelting smooth yarn, such as cotton or acrylic (do not use rayon)

Size F/5 (3.75 mm) crochet hook

72 Pietersite Pebble Chip beads (A)

64 Picture Jasper Chip beads (B)

10 (11 mm) Sea Urchin Shell beads (C)

9 (18 mm) round wooden beads

2 clear seed beads

3 yd clear nylon beading cord

1 gold hook and ring clasp

2 gold knot covers

Needle-nose or chain-nose pliers

Flexible beading needle

Tapestry needle

Jeweler's glue

Shown: Cascade Yarns 220 (100% Peruvian Highland wool; 220 yds (201 m) per 100 g hank): #9421 Turquoise, 1 hank; Fire Mountain Gems and Beads Sea Urchin Shell beads, Picture Jasper Chip beads, Pietersite Pebble Chip beads, and gold hook and ring clasp

Gauge

No specific gauge necessary

125

Crochet Bead (Make 9)

Ch 6. Join with sl st into first ch to form a circle.

Rnd 1: Ch 1, work 6 sc into center of circle, sl st into first sc to join.

Rnd 2: Ch 1, *2 sc into sc, sc in next sc*; rep from * to * two times more, sl st into first sc to join—9 sc rem.

Rnd 3: Ch 1, *sc in 2 sc, 2 sc in next sc*; rep from * to * two times more, sl st into first sc to join—12 sc rem.

Rnd 4: Ch 1, sc in each sc, sl st into first sc to join.

Rnd 5: Ch 1; working in front loop only, *sc in 2 sc, scdec*; rep from * to * two times more, sl st into first sc to join—9 sc rem.

Fit crocheted cup over wooden bead making sure the bead hole is in line with the opening of the beg crocheted circle.

Rnd 6: Ch 1; working in front loop only, *scdec, sc in next sc*; rep from * to * two times more—6 sc rem. Fasten off. Weave in ends.

Hand-Felting

Pull a nonfelting yarn through the center hole of the crochet-covered wooden bead to keep the fabric from shifting during the felting process. Tie the ends of this nonfelting yarn into a knot (see right). Prepare a tub of hot water (as hot as you can stand it wearing rubber gloves) and a tub of ice water. Apply liquid dish soap to the bead and briskly rub the fabric in the hot water. Add more agitation by using a stiff-bristled brush such as a kitchen or a nail brush. Or even rub two beads together. Continue to rub the beads, alternating between the hot and cold water baths. When the fabric has felted sufficiently, rinse well. Squeeze out excess water with a towel. Allow bead to dry completely on a screen mesh or a wire rack for air flow.

126

Stringing Necklace

Cut three lengths of clear nylon beading cord, each 36" (91.5 cm) long. Knotting all three lengths tog and holding them as one, prepare beg end by sliding on seed bead and knot cover, using flexible beading needle (see page 70).

Holding all three cords tog, slide on 1 of each bead in this order: A, C, A.

Remove nonfelting yarn from a crochet bead and slide 1 crochet bead onto beading cords.

*Separate the 3 cords. On each one, randomly slide on 5 of each: A and B.

Holding all 3 cords tog, slide on 1 crochet bead, then slide on 1 of each in this order: C, A, B, A, C, crochet bead*. Rep from * to * once.

**Holding all 3 cords tog, slide on 1 of each in this order: C, A, B, A, C, crochet bead.

Separate the 3 cords. On each one, randomly slide on 5 of each: A and B.

Holding all 3 cords tog, slide on crochet bead**. Rep from ** to ** once.

Slide on 1 of each bead in this order: A, C, A.

Finish off necklace by sliding on another knot cover in opposite direction from the first one (see page 71). Slide on 1 clear seed bead and insert needle through bead again. Move seed bead and knot cover next to the last bead.

Knot all three cords tog, trim and apply jeweler's glue to cut ends.

Close the knot covers using needle-nose or chain-nose pliers around the jump rings on clasp.

127

Garnish with a Twist

On the Cutting Edge

Crocheted edgings are so much fun! Lacy and elegant or fun and flirty, edgings are the delicious icing on the cake, the finishing touch. Edgings can be crocheted directly onto the piece as it's being worked, or they can be crocheted separately and added on later. There are good reasons for using either method. Adding the edging to the piece as you crochet saves time. This method also facilitates correct measurements of the edging. Working the edging separately means that you have to sew or glue the trimming to the main piece. It's also important to make sure the edging piece is the correct length. This second method is particularly useful when you want to add an edging to an existing piece or apply an edging to a garment in a way that doesn't follow the stitch direction (such as on a diagonal, when the larger piece has been worked horizontally).

Edgings don't have to be added to the literal edge of your piece. We've chosen to apply edgings in three unusual locations: the center of the fabric (Pink Panties [opposite]), connected around in a pattern to cover a piece (Topaz Cocktail Bag [page 139]), and made to stand on its own (Black-and-White Martini Necklace and Earrings Set [page 135]).

Edgings come in all sizes, shapes, and flavors, so go ahead and indulge yourself. Edgings . . . 100% fat free and 100% fabulous!

128

Pink Panties

ream up this luxurious pair of panties. Oh so soft and super-fun to make, these undies are an instant favorite. The ruffles on the back side are crocheted directly into the awaiting front loops from previous rows. Adding to the playfulness, chiffon ribbon laces the front and back panels together at the sides.

REFRESH
Loops of a stitch
(page 22)

Finished Size

XSmall (Small, Medium, Large)—26 (30, 34, 38)" [66 (76, 86.5, 96.5) cm] hip measurement
Note: Each finished size may be increased 4" (10 cm) by adjusting the ribbon ties at hips.
Size shown: XSmall—26" (66 cm)

Ingredients

269 (303, 365, 446) yds [246 (277, 334, 408) m] fine-weight 100% alpaca yarn

Size C/2 (2.75 mm) crochet hook, or size to obtain gauge

2 yds (1.83 m) ⅞" (2.2 cm) -wide pink chiffon ribbon

Tapestry needle

Shown: Blue Sky Alpacas Royal (100% alpaca; 288 yds [263 m] per 100 g hank):
#706 Petticoat, 1 (2, 2, 2) hanks

Gauge

24 dc = 4" (10 cm)
4 dc rows = 1¼" (3 cm)
Don't free-pour; do a gauge swatch!

Back

Ch 88 (104, 120, 136).
Row 1: Sl st into eighth ch from hook, *ch 3, skip 3 chs, sl st into next ch*; rep from * to * 19 (23, 27, 31) more times. Do not turn.

Row 2: Rotating piece as if working into free loops of ch and working into ch-3 spaces, sl st into first ch-3 space, ch 3 (counts as first dc of row), 6 dc in same ch-3 space, *skip next ch-3 space, 7 dc in next ch-3 space*; rep from * to * 9 (11, 13, 15) more times. Ch 3, turn.
Rows 3–5: Dc in each dc across— 77 (91, 105, 119) sts rem. Ch 3, turn.
Row 6 (Ruffle Row [RS]): Dc in 15 dc; working in back loop only dc in next 45 (59, 73, 87) dc; working in both loops dc in next 16 dc. Ch 3, turn.
Rows 7–9: Dc in each dc across. Ch 3, turn.

Row 10 (Ruffle Row): Dc in 10 dc; working in back loop only dc in next 55 (69, 83, 97) dc; working in both loops dc in next 11 dc. Ch 3, turn.

Row 11: Dc in each dc across. Ch 3, turn.

Rows 12 and 13: (Dcdec) twice, dc across to last 4 dc, (dcdec) twice—69 (83, 97, 111) sts at end of row 13—(ch-3 counts as first dc and each dc dec counts as 1 dc). Ch 3, turn.

Row 14 (Ruffle Row): (Dcdec) twice, dc in next 7 dc; working in back loop only dc in next 46 (60, 74, 88) dc; working in both loops dc in

next 7 dc; (dcdec) twice (work last half of last dcdec into ch 3)—65 (79, 93, 107) sts rem. Ch 3, turn.

Rows 15–17: (Dcdec) twice, dc across to last 4 dc, (dcdec) twice—53 (67, 81, 95) sts rem at end of row 17. Ch 3, turn.

Row 18 (Ruffle Row): (Dcdec) twice, dc in next 6 dc; working in back loop only dc in next 32 (46, 60, 74) dc; working in both loops dc in next 6 dc, (dcdec) twice—49 (63, 77, 91) sts rem. Ch 3, turn.

Rows 19–21: (Dcdec) twice, dc across to last 4 dc, (dcdec) twice—37 (51, 65, 79) sts rem at end of row 21. Ch 3, turn.

Row 22 (Ruffle Row): (Dcdec) twice, dc in next 5 dc; working into back loop only dc in next 18 (32, 46, 60) dc; working in both loops dc in next 5 dc, (dcdec) twice—33 (47, 61, 75) sts rem. Ch 3, turn.

Rows 23–27: (Dcdec) twice, dc across to last 4 dc, (dcdec) twice—13 (27, 41, 55) sts rem. Ch 3, turn. For size XSmall only, omit ch-3 turn at end of row 27 and fasten off.

For Sizes Small (Medium, Large) Only:

Rows 28–30: (Dcdec) twice, dc across to last 4 dc, (dcdec) twice—0 (15, 29, 43) sts rem. Ch 3, turn. For size Small only, omit ch-3 at end of row 30 and fasten off.

For Sizes Medium (Large) Only:

Rows 31–33: (Dcdec) twice, dc across to last 4 dc, (dcdec) twice—0

(0, 17, 31) sts rem. Ch 3, turn. For size Medium only, omit ch-3 at end of row 33 and fasten off.

For Size Large Only:

Rows 34–36: (Dcdec) twice, dc across to last 4 dc, (dcdec) twice—0 (0, 0, 19) sts rem. Ch 3, turn. Omit ch-3 at end of row 36 and fasten off.

Front

Ch 88 (104, 120, 136).

Rep rows 1 and 2 from back.

Rows 3–10: Dc in each dc across—77 (91, 105, 119) sts rem. Ch 3, turn.

Row 11: Dc in 4 dc, sc in next 14 (18, 22, 26) sts, dc in 39 (45, 51, 57) dc, sc in next 14 (18, 22, 26) sts, dc in 5 dc. Ch 1, turn.

Row 12 (Leg Shaping): Sc in first st and next st, sl st in next 16 (20, 24, 28) sts, sc in next st, dc in 37 (43, 49, 55) dc, sc in next st, sl st in next 16 (20, 24, 28) sts, sc in last 3 sts. Fasten off. Ch 1, turn work as usual.

Row 13 (Dec center section): With WS facing, attach yarn to the first dc of the center section, sc in next dc, dc in next 32 (38, 44, 50) dc; sc in next dc, sl st in next dc—35 (41, 47, 53) sts rem. Ch 1, turn.

Row 14: Sl st in sc, sc in dc, dc in next dc, dcdec, dc in next 22 (28, 34, 40) dc, dcdec, dc in next dc, sc in dc, sl st in next dc—30 (36, 42, 48) sts rem. Ch 1, turn.

Row 15: Sl st into sc, sc in dc, dc in 23 (29, 35, 41) dc, sc in dc, sl st into dc—27 (33, 39, 45) sts rem. Ch 1, turn.

Row 16: Sl st into sc, sc in dc, dc in next dc, dcdec, dc in 14 (20, 26, 32) dc, dcdec, dc in next dc, sc in dc, sl st into dc—22 (28, 34, 40) sts rem. Ch 1, turn.

For Size XSmall Only:

Proceed to instructions "For All Sizes."

For Sizes Small (Medium, Large) Only:

Row 17: Sl st into sc, sc in dc, dc in 22 (28, 34) dc, sc in dc, sl st in sc—26 (32, 38) sts rem. Ch 1, turn.

Row 18: Sl st into sc, sc in dc, dc in next dc, dcdec, dc in 14 (20, 26) dc, dcdec, dc in next dc, sc in dc, sl st in sc—22 (28, 34) sts rem. Ch 1, turn. For size Small only, proceed to instructions "For All Sizes."

For Sizes Medium (Large) Only:

Rows 19 and 20: Rep rows 17 and 18.

For size Medium, proceed to instructions "For All Sizes."

For Size Large Only:

Rows 21 and 22: Rep rows 17 and 18. Proceed to instructions "For All Sizes."

For All Sizes:

Next row: Skip sc, sc in dc, dc in 15 dc, sc in dc, sl st into dc—18 sts rem. Ch 3, turn.

Next row: Dc in sc, dc in 15 dc—17 sts rem. Ch 3, turn.

Next 16 rows: 16 dc—17 sts rem. Do not fasten off.

First Ruffle

Row 1: With RS facing back and fabric turned so that the beg ch is down, pull up loop into the free front loop of row 6, ch 3, 1 dc in same front loop, *3 dc in next front loop, 2 dc in next dc*; rep from * to * across. Ch 4, turn.

Row 2: Tr in each dc across. Fasten off.

Second Ruffle

Rep rows 1 and 2 of first ruffle in row 10.

Third Ruffle

Rep rows 1 and 2 of first ruffle in row 14.

Fourth Ruffle

Rep rows 1 and 2 of first ruffle in row 18.

Fifth Ruffle

Rep rows 1 and 2 of first ruffle in row 22.

Finishing

Hold front and back pieces with WS facing each other. Center the pieces with each other.

Ch 1, sl st into front loop only of front piece and back loop only of back piece, matching st for st (first st of front to first st of back). Continue sl st the front and back tog across row. Fasten off.

Weave in ends. Cut ribbon in half, each piece 1 yd (91.5 cm) long, and thread each ribbon (as if lacing shoes) through the side edges of front and back. Tie in bows.

It may help when working the ruffles to fold the fabric at each ruffle row so that the front loops are easier to crochet into.

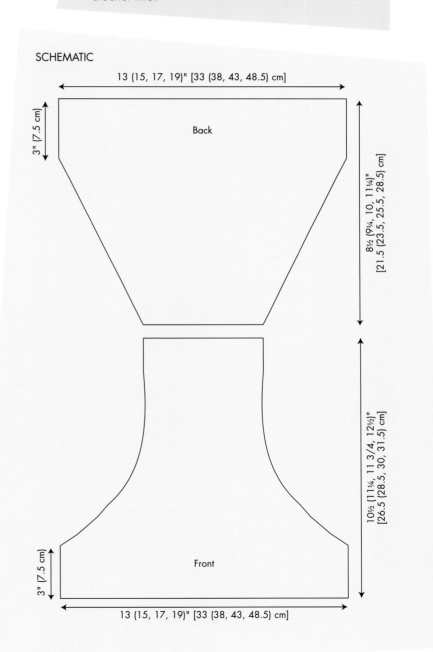

SCHEMATIC

13 (15, 17, 19)" [33 (38, 43, 48.5) cm]

3" (7.5 cm)

Back

8½ (9¼, 10, 11¼)" [21.5 (23.5, 25.5, 28.5) cm]

10½ (11¼, 11 3/4, 12½)" [26.5 (28.5, 30, 31.5) cm]

3" (7.5 cm)

Front

13 (15, 17, 19)" [33 (38, 43, 48.5) cm]

133

Black-and-White Martini Necklace and Earrings Set

Inspired by a Victorian silver vanity set, this delicate set of necklace and earrings are sophisticated. Light dances off of the faceted teardrop crystals, while the metallic thread sparkles. If you've never worked with a steel crochet hook, now's your chance. These pieces are small enough to give you a quick taste, and the resulting necklace and earrings are enchanting.

135

Finished Size

Necklace: 16" (40.5 cm) long
Earrings: 1¼" (3 cm) long (not including earring wires)

Ingredients

25 yds (23 m) super fine–weight metallic type yarn 🪢1

Size 10 (1.15 mm) steel crochet hook

31 (11 × 5.5 mm) black teardrop crystal beads

1 large silver filigree clasp

2 silver earring wires

Beading needle

Embroidery needle

Jeweler's glue

Shown: South West Trading Company Shimmer (50% nylon, 50% polyester; 150 yds [137 m] per 25 g ball): #405 Silver, 1 ball; Swarovski 11 × 5.5 mm teardrop crystals in Jet

Gauge

(picot, bead drop, picot) = ¾" (2 cm)
Don't free-pour; do a gauge swatch!

Stitch Explanation

Picot—ch 6, sl st into sc just worked

Ch 1 bead—slide bead up to hook, yarn over hook and pull through loop on hook to secure bead

Bead drop—ch 6, ch 1 bead, ch 6

Tip

When crocheting with super-fine yarn, help keep tension in check by wrapping the thread around your pinkie before wrapping it around your index finger.

Necklace

Slide 29 teardrop crystals onto yarn before beg.

Ch 151, leaving a 6" (15 cm) tail. Sc into second ch from hook and into each ch across—150 sc. Ch 1, turn.

Sc in 1st sc and in next 2 sc, *picot, sc in next 2 sc, bead drop, sc into next 3 sc*; rep from * to * 28 more times, picot, sc in last 2 sc. Fasten off.

Slip one half of clasp onto 6" (15 cm) tail onto a fastened-off end. Tie knot. Rep with other clasp half on opposite end of necklace.

Weave in ends. Apply jeweler's glue to cut ends.

Earrings

Slide 1 teardrop crystal onto yarn before beg.

Ch 9, sc into second ch from hook and into next 2 chs, ch 6, sl st into sc just worked, sc in next ch, bead drop, sc in next 2 chs, ch 6, sl st into sc just worked, sc in last 2 sc, sl st into beg sc. Fasten off.

Use beg and ending tails to tie knot through loop at base of earring wire. Weave in ends. Apply jeweler's glue to cut ends.

Rep for second earring.

137

Topaz Cocktail Bag

This beautiful drawstring purse adds a touch of sophistication and elegance, the perfect garnish to a night at the ballet. Relax with easy single crochet and a beautiful silk yarn, then challenge yourself with a jewel-shaped edging that is attached at intervals to the single crochet rows.

Note: The purse is crocheted at a tighter gauge than you might be accustomed to. Stick to the gauge listed; the tighter gauge creates a firm fabric for your purse, so you don't lose your lipstick while you're dancing the night away.

REFRESH
Crocheting around post (page 23)
Crocheting in the round (page 40)

Finished Size

Approx 15" (38 cm) circumference × 7½" (19 cm) high

Ingredients

240 yds (219.5 m) medium-weight silk yarn (4)

Size F/5 (3.75 mm) crochet hook, or size to obtain gauge

Tapestry needle

Shown: Tilli Tomas Simply Heaven (100% spun silk; approx 120 yds [109.7 m] per hank): #152 Rattan, 2 hank

Gauge

16 sts = 4" (10 cm) in sc before edging
16 rnds = 4" (10 cm) in sc before edging
Don't free-pour; do a gauge swatch!

Base of Purse

Ch 3. Sl st in ch to form ring.
Rnd 1: Ch 1, 6 sc in ring. Sl st in first sc to join.
Rnd 2: Ch 1, 2 sc in each sc around—12 sc rem. Sl st in first sc to join.
Rnd 3: Ch 1, *sc in next sc, 2 sc in next sc*; rep from * to * around—18 sc rem. Sl st in first sc to join.
Rnd 4: Ch 1, *sc in next 2 sc, 2 sc in next sc*; rep from * to * around—24 sc rem. Sl st in first sc to join.
Rnd 5: Ch 1, *sc in next 3 sc, 2 sc in next sc*; rep from * to * around—30 sc rem. Sl st in first sc to join.

Rnd 6: Ch 1, *sc in next 4 sc, 2 sc in next sc*; rep from * to * around—36 sc rem. Sl st in first sc to join.

Rnd 7: Ch 1, *sc in next 5 sc, 2 sc in next sc*; rep from * to * around—42 sc rem. Sl st in first sc to join.

Rnd 8: Ch 1, *sc in next 6 sc, 2 sc in next sc*; rep from * to * around—48 sc rem. Sl st in first sc to join.

Rnd 9: Ch 1, *sc in next 7 sc, 2 sc in next sc*; rep from * to * around—54 sc rem. Sl st in first sc to join.

Rnd 10: Ch 1, *sc in next 8 sc, 2 sc in next sc*; rep from * to * around— 60 sc rem. Sl st in first sc to join.

Fasten off.

Body of Purse

Ch 60. Sl st into first ch to join, being careful not to twist.

Rnd 1: Ch 1, sc in each ch around. Sl st in first sc to join.

Rnds 2–20: Ch 1, sc in each sc around. Sl st in first sc to join.

Rnd 21: Ch 1, *sc in next 8 sc, sc dec*; rep from * to * around, sl st in first sc to join—54 sc.

Rnd 22: Ch 1, sc in each sc around. Sl st in first sc to join.

Rnd 23: Ch 1, *sc in next 7 sc, sc dec*; rep from * to * around—48 sc.

Rnds 24–25: Ch 1, sc in each sc around. Sl st in first sc to join.

Rnd 26 (Eyelet for Drawstring): Ch 3, skip first 3 sc, *sc into next sc, ch 2, skip next 2 sc*; rep from * to * around. End with sl st in first ch of ch 3.

Rnd 27: Ch 1, sc into same st as sl st, *2 sc into ch-2 space, sc into next sc*; rep from * to * around—48 sc rem. Sl st in first sc to join.

Rnds 28–30: Ch 1, sc in each sc around. Sl st in first sc to join.

Fasten off.

Jewel Edging

Rnd 1 (Edging): Turn work upside down. Rnd 1 of body of purse should now be at the top of your work. Count to fifth rnd from base of purse, and attach yarn to this rnd as follows: Insert hook under post of first st, wrap yarn around hook, then pull yarn through to create the first loop. Secure yarn tail. Counting the sc used to attach yarn as first st, *sl st around post of first 4 sc of this rnd; work (sl st, ch 5, sl st) around post of next sc. You have created a

Tips

- To keep from accidentally migrating to the next row when adding each row of edging, place stitch markers at 2" to 3" (5 to 7.5 cm) intervals around the post of stitches on that row to guide yourself.

- When working the loops for the edging, it is very important that you remember to turn your work after slip-stitching, to secure the loop to the sides. If you don't, your loops will twist and won't lay flat.

140

loop, and will now work back and forth on this loop. Ch 1, turn. Work 9 sc into loop just created, sl st into the fourth sl st from beg (or last "jewel" worked) to secure edge of loop to body of purse. Ch 1, turn. Continue working into same "jewel" as follows: Sc into third st from hook, then sc into next 3 sc, (sc, ch 3, sc) into next sc, sc into rem 4 sc of loop—1 "jewel" completed*; rep from * to * around—12 "jewels" made. Sl st into first st. Fasten off.

Rnd 2: With work still upside down, count to fifth rnd from edging rnd 1 (10 rnds from base of purse). Attach yarn as for edging rnd 1. Sl st around post of first sc of rnd, *(sl st, ch 5, sl st) into post of next sc. You have created a loop, and you will be working back and forth on this loop. Ch 1, turn. Work 9 sc into loop just created; sl st into the previously made sl st closest to end of loop (fourth sl st from beg of last "jewel" worked) to secure edge of loop to body of purse. Ch 1, turn. Sc into third st from hook, then sc into next 3 sc, (sc, ch 3, sc) into next sc, sc into rem 4 sc of loop, sl st around post of next 4 scs*; rep from * to * around, ending with sl st around post of next 3 sts (12 "jewels" made). Fasten off.

Rnd 3: With work still upside down, count 5 rows down from edging rnd 2. Rep as for edging rnd 1.

Rnd 4: With work still upside down, count 5 rows down from edging rnd 3. Rep as for edging rnd 2.

Drawstring

Ch 133. Turn ch so that the bumps of ch are facing you. Sl st into second bump from hook and each bump across—132 sl sts.

Fasten off, leaving a 6" (15 cm) tail.

Thread drawstring through eyelets at top of purse. Pull 6" (15 cm) tail through opposite end of drawstring and secure, so that drawstring is now one continuous loop.

Finishing

With RS facing, sc bottom of purse body and purse base together. Beginning with first st of the last round of base and bottom bump of ch from purse body, sc both together. Continue around, working st for st. Weave in all loose ends. Lightly press (use pressing cloth and low setting on iron) so that "jewels" of edging lay flat against the sc stitch fabric.

141

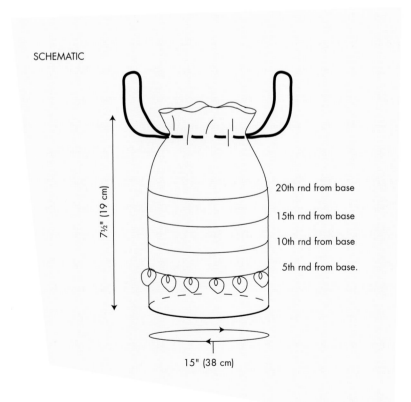

SCHEMATIC

7½" (19 cm)

20th rnd from base

15th rnd from base

10th rnd from base

5th rnd from base.

15" (38 cm)

Cheers!

Throw Your Own Yarn Cocktails Party

Statistically, we spend more and more time working and commuting, leaving less time for relaxation and socializing. Crocheting is by nature a community activity, so gather your friends together for a fun and relaxing evening of crocheting by hosting your own *Yarn Cocktails* party.

The key ingredients to a *Yarn Cocktails* party are good food, good friends, and some good yarn. After that, the theme can be extended as far as you wish.

When preparing a menu for a *Yarn Cocktails* party, select foods that your guests can enjoy with their crochet. Finger foods such as fresh fruit or cheese served with toothpicks will allow your guests to stab their food and keep their hands clean. For fun, put toothpicks in bite-size meatballs,

to represent balls of yarn with a hook. It doesn't hurt to have moist tow-elettes on hand, just in case. A skein of licorice laces tangled together with some crochet hooks makes a conversation piece that your guests will enjoy unraveling or perhaps even crocheting. You may choose to extend the *Yarn Cocktails* theme to include drinks. Recipes for the drinks that inspired the patterns in this book are included on pages 144–147. A word of warning: as the host, you are responsible for the safety of your guests. Think yarn over, not hangover! Encourage your guests to drink responsibly, and if guests do imbibe, do not let them drive. Your intervention could save a life.

Present your guests with a smorgasbord of yarns. Arrange a variety of

small balls of coordinating yarns in large cocktail glasses. Invite each guest to select a ball from each glass and a crochet hook and swatch away. Sew each swatch together into a scarf, then hold a drawing for the finished scarf. The winner keeps the scarf as a memento of the party.

For a fun game, hold a fastest-crocheter competition. Turn this competition into a great charity activity by choosing an easy hat or scarf pattern. Challenge your guests to crochet as many as they can during the party, then donate the finished items to a favorite charity.

Everyone loves a goody bag. Stuff it with inexpensive, useful favors such as row counters, stitch markers, coil-less safety pins, and needle gauges.

Recipes

Here are some cocktail recipes, so go stir up some fun!

CHAPTER 1
Classic Cocktails

Brandy Alexander

1 ounce (30 ml) cream

1 ounce (30 ml) crème de cacao

1 ounce (30 ml) brandy

Ground nutmeg, for garnish

Pour all ingredients into a shaker with ice cubes. Shake well. Strain into a chilled cocktail glass and garnish with a dusting of nutmeg.

Classic Sidecar

1½ ounces (42 ml) cognac

¾ ounce (23 ml) orange liqueur

¼ ounce (7 ml) lemon juice

Pour the ingredients into a shaker with ice cubes. Shake well. Strain into a chilled cocktail glass.

Bourbon and Cola

1–2 ounces (30–60 ml) bourbon whiskey

Cola

Lemon slice, for garnish

Fill a highball glass with lots of ice and pour in the whiskey. Add the cola. Decorate with a slice of lemon.

42nd Street

1 ounce (30 ml) bourbon whiskey

1 ounce (15 ml) orange liqueur

½ ounce (15 ml) dry vermouth

Lemon peel, for garnish

Maraschino cherry, for garnish

Stir all ingredients with ice. Strain into a cocktail glass.

CHAPTER 2
Frozen Drinks

Frozen Mint

½ ounce (15 ml) white crème de menthe

½ ounce (15 ml) coffee liqueur

½ ounce (15 ml) crème de cacao

½ ounce (15 ml) Irish cream

1½ (44 ml) ounces milk

2 scoops vanilla ice cream

Whipped cream, for garnish

Maraschino cherry, for garnish

Combine all ingredients in a blender. Blend until smooth and slightly thick. Pour into a collins glass with a few ice cubes. Garnish with whipped cream and a maraschino cherry. Add straws, and serve.

144

Floridita

1½ ounces (44 ml) white rum

¾ ounce (23 ml) vermouth

2–3 dashes white crème de cacao

Dash of grenadine syrup

½ ounce (15 ml) lime juice

Combine all ingredients. Pour over ice in a shaker. Shake well. Strain into a chilled cocktail glass.

Royal Peach Freeze

3 ounces (90 ml) orange juice

2 ounces (60 ml) peach schnapps

½ ounce (15 ml) lime juice

1½ ounces (42 ml) dry sparkling white wine

Blend all but the wine in a blender with 3 ounces of crushed ice. Pour into a wine goblet and add the wine. Stir and serve.

Raspberry Margarita

1 pint (300 g) fresh raspberries

½ lime

6 ounces (177 ml) tequila

3 ounces (90 ml) triple sec

1 tablespoon (15 g) sugar

Liquefy the raspberries in a blender. Add the remaining ingredients, top with ice, and blend smooth. Taste, and add sugar if you like. Serve in a margarita glass with a sugar-coated rim.

CHAPTER 3
Champagne Drinks

Champagne Polonaise

4 ounces (118 ml) champagne

½ ounce (15 ml) blackberry brandy

¼ ounce (7 ml) honey liqueur

Combine the champagne, brandy, and liqueur in a champagne flute. Serve.

Ritz Cocktail

¾ ounce (23 ml) cognac

¼ ounce (7 ml) orange liqueur

¾ ounce (23 ml) orange juice

3 ounces (90 ml) champagne

Shake the cognac, orange liqueur, and orange juice over ice cubes. Strain into a champagne flute, carefully fill with champagne, and serve.

Champagne Charlie

2 ounces (60 ml) apricot brandy

Chilled champagne

Pour the apricot brandy into a champagne flute and top it off with chilled champagne.

Mimosa

2 ounces (60 ml) orange juice

Chilled champagne

Pour the orange juice into champagne flute. Fill with champagne and stir gently.

CHAPTER 4
Tropical Drinks

Bay Blue

1½ ounces (42 ml) vodka

1½ ounces (42 ml) blueberry schnapps

2 ounces (60 ml) lemon-lime soda

2 ounces (60 ml) cranberry juice

1 splash Blue Curaçao

Pour the vodka, schnapps, and soda into a highball glass. Then slowly add the cranberry juice. Float the Blue Curaçao on top. If done right, you'll have a nice multicolored drink.

Casablanca

2 ounces (60 ml) light rum

1 ounce (30 ml) apricot brandy

1 ounce (30 ml) lime juice

1 ounce (30 ml) orange liqueur

1 teaspoon (5 ml) maraschino liqueur

Shake all ingredients with ice. Strain into a cocktail glass and serve.

Malibu Bay Breeze

1½ ounces (42 ml) rum

2 ounces (60 ml) cranberry juice

2 ounces (60 ml) pineapple juice

Mix all ingredients and pour in to a cocktail glass over ice.

Ocean View

1 ounce (30 ml) vodka

⅓ ounce (10 ml) dry vermouth

⅓ ounce (10 ml) melon liqueur

⅓ ounce (10 ml) Blue Curaçao

Lemon twist, for garnish

Stir with ice and strain into a cocktail glass. Garnish with a lemon twist.

CHAPTER 5
Martini Drinks

Sweet Vodka Martini

1 ounce (30 ml) vodka

¾ ounce (23 ml) banana liqueur

¾ ounce (23 ml) melon liqueur

Whipped cream, for garnish (optional)

Maraschino cherry, for garnish (optional)

Combine the vodka and liqueurs in a shaker filled with ice. Stir, then strain into cocktail glass. If desired, top with whipped cream and a maraschino cherry.

Blueberry Martini

3 ounces (90 ml) gin

1 splash raspberry liqueur

1 splash Blue Curaçao liqueur

Pour all ingredients into a chilled martini glass, stir to combine, and serve.

Palm Beach Cocktail

1½ ounces (42 ml) gin

1½ teaspoons (7 ml) sweet vermouth

1½ teaspoons (7 ml) grapefruit juice

Shake all ingredients with ice, strain into a cocktail glass, and serve.

Bentley Martini

1 ounce (30 ml) applejack

1 ounce (30 ml) wine-based aperatif or quinquina

Shake all ingredients with ice, strain into a cocktail glass, and serve.

CHAPTER 6
Coffee Drinks

Chambord Coffee

1 ounce (30 ml) raspberry liqueur

5 ounces (150 ml) hot black coffee

1½ ounces (42 g) whipped cream

1 teaspoon (4 g) sugar

Raspberry, for garnish

Pour the coffee and liqueur into an Irish coffee cup and sweeten to taste. Float the cream on top, garnish with a fresh raspberry, and serve.

Caribbean Coffee

1 ounce (30 ml) dark rum

1 ounce (30 ml) crème de cacao

Hot coffee

Ground cinnamon, for garnish

Cinnamon stick, for garnish

Whipped cream, for garnish

Pour the rum and crème de cacao into a sugar-rimmed Irish coffee glass. Fill with coffee and top with whipped cream. Sprinkle with cinnamon. Add a cinnamon stick to stir.

Baja Coffee

2 tablespoons (22 g) grated semisweet chocolate

3 tablespoons (30 g) instant coffee

½ cup (120 ml) coffee liqueur

1½ ounces (42 g) whipped cream

2 ounces (60 ml) crème de cacao

8 cups (2 L) hot water

Whipped cream, for garnish

Grated chocolate, for garnish

In slow cooker, combine the hot water, coffee, and liqueurs. Cover and heat over low heat for 2 to 4 hours. Ladle into mugs or heatproof glasses. Top with whipped cream and grated chocolate. Serves about 10.

CHAPTER 7
Garnish with a Twist

Pink Panties

1 10-ounce (295 ml) package frozen pink lemonade concentrate

8 ounces (235 ml) whiskey

8 ounces (235 ml) water

½ container whipped cream

Combine all ingredients in a blender with half a cup of crushed ice. Blend until smooth. Serve in a tall glass.

Black-and-White Martini

3 ounces (90 ml) vanilla vodka

1 ounce (30 ml) crème de cacao

Black and white licorice candy, for garnish

Half-fill a cocktail shaker with crushed ice. Add the vanilla vodka and crème de cacao. Shake well and strain into a chilled cocktail glass. Garnish with a black and white licorice candy.

Topaz Cocktail

3 ounces (90 ml) scotch

1½ ounces (42 ml) butterscotch schnapps

1 tablespoon (15 ml) Italian herbal liqueur

Combine ingredients in a shaker two-thirds filled with ice. Shake. Strain into a cocktail glass and serve.

Maybe You Need a Refresher Course

Holding Hook and Yarn
Step 1

There are two main ways to hold a crochet hook. One way is to hold it like a pencil, as shown in the top illustration. The other is to hold it overhand like a knife, as shown in the bottom illustration. Use whichever way is most comfortable for you. Many crochet hooks have a flattened area called the grip (see page 10) that is intended as the place to comfortably position your thumb and index finger when holding your hook.

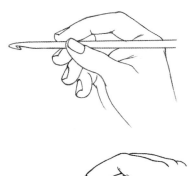

Step 2

The yarn feeding from the ball or hank must be held with slight tension as you crochet. Holding the yarn in your left hand by letting it wrap through your fingers and around your little finger as shown is a good way to maintain this tension.

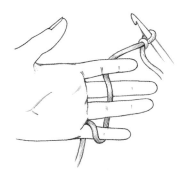

Step 3

With the yarn held in your left hand as shown in the last step, use your index or forefinger, slightly raised, as a guide for the yarn to feed over as shown here. At the same time, use your left middle finger and thumb to hold (similar to pinching) the work that is just below your hook. As you crochet, keep moving your left middle finger and thumb up, so you are always holding the work that is just below your hook.

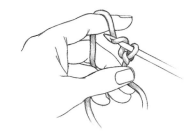

Slip Knot

Step 1

Almost all crochet pieces begin with a foundation chain. To begin this base chain, make a slip knot by looping the yarn and then using the hook to pull another loop through.

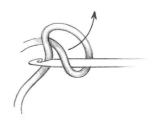

Step 2

With the new loop on your hook, use your left fingers to pull on the tail of the yarn and tighten the slip knot.

Yarn Over (yo)

To yarn over, move the hook under the yarn from left to right and let the yarn catch on the hook as shown. Try to keep the yarn still (by controlling it with your left hand), using your right hand to maneuver the hook to do each yarn over. You can also move the yarn, instead of the hook, to make a yarn over. Bring the yarn over the hook from back to front and let the hook catch the yarn. Yarn overs are done many, many times in crochet, so you will get lots of practice doing them.

Chain Stitch (ch)

Step 1

Yarn over and draw the yarn through the loop on the hook. Be careful not to tighten the previous loop/chain; just bring the new loop through the previous loop. You have just chained one.

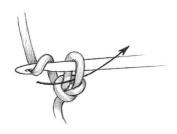

Step 2

To continue the chain stitch, just yarn over and draw through a new loop on the hook again for each chain required. The slip knot does not count as a chain.

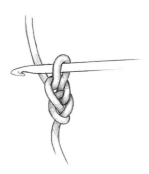

149

Counting Chains

Begin counting chains just above the slip knot. Do not count the slip knot. Count each "v" up to the one before the hook. Do not count the loop on the hook.

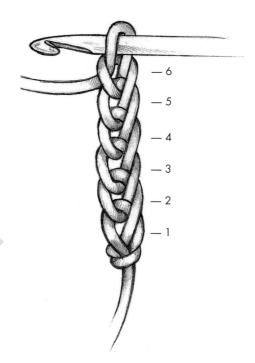

Front and Back of Chains

Notice that when working into each base chain, the hook should be inserted in the middle of the "v" as you will see in the illustration below. This creates a nice, firm starting row. The back of each chain has a bump. Sometimes you are asked to work into the back bump of each chain. This results in a nicely finished edge.

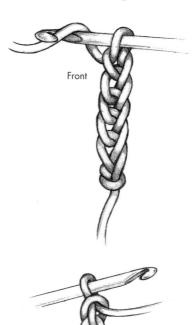

Front

Back

Slip Stitch (sl st)

The slip stitch is the shortest of the crochet stitches. It is often used for joining, shaping, and seaming. Seaming with a sl st gives a firm, finished edge. Insert the hook into the stitch, yarn over, and pull the yarn through the stitch and the loop on the hook in one movement.

Single Crochet (sc)

Step 1

Single crochet is the next tallest stitch after the slip stitch. Insert the hook into the stitch, *yarn over, and draw through the stitch only. You now have 2 loops on the hook.

Step 2

Yarn over again and draw through both loops on the hook in one movement.

Step 3

The first single crochet is now completed. To continue in single crochet, insert hook into the next stitch and repeat from * in Step 1.

Single Crochet Decrease (scdec)

Step 1

Insert the hook into the stitch, yarn over, and draw through the stitch only. You now have 2 loops on the hook.

Step 2

Insert hook into the next stitch, yarn over, and draw through the stitch only. You now have 3 loops on the hook.

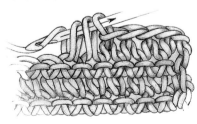

Step 3

Yarn over again and draw through all 3 loops on the hook in one movement. The scdec is complete and counts as one stitch.

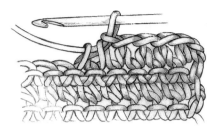

Half Double Crochet (hdc)

Step 1

Half double crochet is the next tallest stitch after the single crochet stitch. Before inserting your hook into the stitch, yarn over. Now insert the hook into the stitch.

Step 2

Yarn over and *pull loop through the stitch only. You will have 3 loops on the hook.

Step 3

Yarn over and pull through all 3 loops on the hook in one movement.

151

Step 4

The first half double crochet is now completed. To continue in half double crochet, yarn over, insert your hook into the next stitch, and repeat from * in Step 2.

Double Crochet (dc)

Step 1

Double crochet is the next tallest stitch and is very, very commonly used in crochet patterns. Before inserting your hook into the stitch, yarn over. Now insert the hook into the stitch.

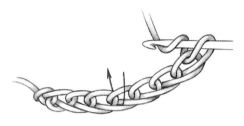

Step 2

*Yarn over and draw through the stitch only. You will have 3 loops on the hook.

Step 3

Yarn over and draw through only the first 2 loops on the hook. You will now have 2 loops remaining on the hook.

Step 4

Yarn over and draw through the remaining 2 loops on the hook.

Step 5

The first double crochet is now completed. To continue in double crochet, yarn over, insert hook into the next stitch, and repeat from * in Step 2.

Double Crochet Decrease (dcdec)

Step 1

Before inserting your hook into the stitch, yarn over. Now insert the hook into the stitch.

Step 2

*Yarn over and draw through the stitch only. You will have 3 loops on the hook.

Step 3

Yarn over and draw through only the first 2 loops on the hook. You will now have 2 loops remaining on the hook.

Step 4

Yarn over and insert hook into next stitch. Yarn over and draw through the stitch only. You will have 4 loops on the hook. Yarn over and draw through only the first 2 loops on hook. You will now have 3 loops on hook.

Step 5

Yarn over and draw through the remaining 3 loops on the hook. The double crochet decrease is complete and counts as one stitch.

Treble Crochet (tr)

Step 1

The treble crochet is the tallest of the basic stitches. Before inserting the hook into the stitch, yarn over twice. Now insert the hook into the stitch.

Step 2

Yarn over and draw through the stitch only. You will have 4 loops on the hook.

Step 3

Yarn over again and draw through only the first 2 loops. You will have 3 loops left on the hook.

Step 4

Yarn over again and draw through only the next 2 loops. You will now have 2 loops remaining on the hook.

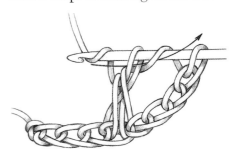

Step 5

Yarn over again and draw through the remaining 2 loops. One treble crochet is now completed.

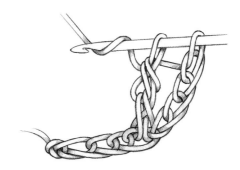

153

Turning the Work

A flat fabric is created by turning the work to the other side after each row is completed. The new row is then worked from right to left on top of the first row. The work is then turned to the first side again, the next row is worked from right to left on top of the second row, and so on.

Each new row begins with the required number of chains to reach the height of the basic stitch used for that row. This is called a beginning, or turning, chain. Generally, the turning chain is counted and treated as one of the stitches for that row for all stitches but the slip stitch and single crochet stitch. After the turning chains have been worked, the pattern may instruct you to "turn." This means to flip the fabric to the other side following the direction of the arrows as shown below.

Turning Rows
Step 1

Here, a basic double crochet fabric is illustrated. The first row was worked into a base chain that had an extra chain 3 to match the height of the double crochet stitches. Therefore, the first double crochet was worked into the fourth chain from the hook (the first 3 skipped chains are counted as 1 double crochet stitch). Then, a double crochet was worked into each chain across to the end.

Step 2

At the end of the row, turn the work to the opposite side. Three chains were made for the turning chain in this example to match the height of the double crochets. The first double crochet from the previous row will be skipped since the turning chain will be treated as the first double crochet. Use one chain to turn single crochet work, two chains to turn half double crochet work, and three chains to turn double crochet work. For a tighter turn, two chains may also be used to turn double crochet work.

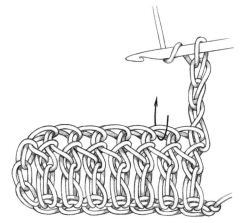

Step 3

Skipping the first double crochet in the previous row, 1 double crochet is then worked into each stitch across. The last double crochet of the row is worked into the top chain of the 3 chains that were from the beginning of the previous row. This is often written in instructions as working "1 double crochet into the top of the turning chain." When working into a chain from the previous row, be sure to pick up 2 strands of yarn as shown.

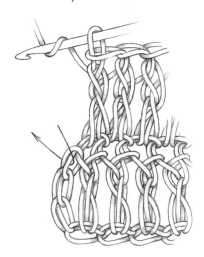

Changing Yarns/Colors
Step 1

When it is time to change colors, lay your new color across your work, on top of the next stitch. Leave at least a 6" (15 cm) tail; you'll weave this in later. Work the first part of the stitch with the old color. When two loops remain on your hook, yarn over with the new color and pull through these two loops to finish the stitch.

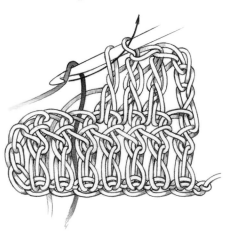

Step 2

Be sure to leave at least a 6" (15 cm) tail before cutting old yarn to weave in later. Or, if you prefer, weave in as you go by crocheting over those 6" (15 cm) tails: lay the tails over the top of your stitches, then insert the hook in to the next stitch and under 6" (15 cm) tail and complete stitch as usual.

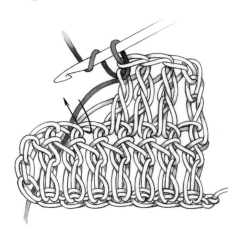

155

Fasten Off

Step 1

Crochet is fastened off with a final chain. In this example, it is done after the final round has been joined with the slip stitch. The yarn is then cut, leaving at least a 6" (15 cm) tail and pulled through the final loop. This tail will be woven into the fabric when finishing the project.

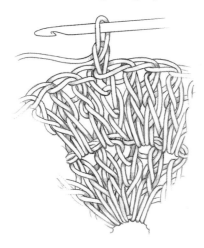

Step 2

Gently pull the tail to tighten.

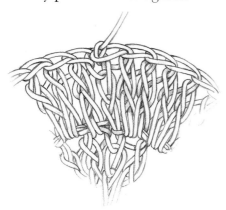

Woven Seam

With the fabrics lying flat and right sides facing you, place their edges together. Pin them together every few inches to keep the pieces from shifting. Thread a tapestry needle with a length of yarn and insert it down and up through the edge of the left piece of fabric. Then, insert it in the same way through the edge of the right piece of fabric. Keep alternating from left to right, and pull the yarn only enough to snug the edges together. There should be no puckering or holes.

Whip Stitch

Place the edges of the two fabrics together. If sewing a side seam that is not meant to show, place the right sides of the fabrics facing each other. Pin them together every few inches to keep the pieces from shifting. Thread a tapestry needle with a

length of yarn and insert it through the edge stitches of both layers. Pull and bring the yarn around to the front. Insert the needle through both layers again in the same way.

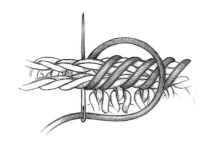

Weave in Ends

After fastening off, hide the yarn tail by threading a tapestry needle and inserting it into the the wrong side of the crocheted fabric in an up-and-down "weaving" motion. Do this for a couple of inches (or cm), give the yarn a little tug, and cut. The cut end will be hidden within the stitches.

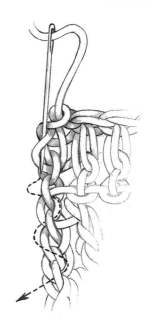

Resources

Thirsty for more? Look for *Yarn Cocktails* purse-size patterns at your local yarn shop. To find a shop near you, see the Store Locator at www.anastasiaknits.com, home of *Yarn Cocktails* designs.

Check out these fantastic companies that produce luscious yarns, beads, and other great products. They graciously provided supplies for the projects in this book.

Alpaca with a Twist
4272 Evans Jacobi Road
Georgetown, IN 47122-9708 USA
(866) 378-9478
www.alpacawithatwist.com

The Alpaca Yarn Company
144 Roosevelt Avenue Bay #1
York, PA 17401 USA
(866) 440-PACA
www.thealpacayarnco.com

Berroco
P.O. Box 367
Uxbridge, MA 01569 USA
(508) 278-2527
www.berroco.com

Blue Heron Yarns
29532 Canvasback Drive, Suite #6
Easton, MD 21601 USA
(410) 819-0401
www.blueheronyarns.com

Blue Sky Alpacas
P.O. Box 88
Cedar, MN 55011 USA
www.blueskyalpacas.com

Bull's Eye Buttons
P.O. Box 1416
Chautauqua, NY 14722 USA
www.bullseyebutton.com

Cascade Yarns
1224 Andover Park E
Tukwila, WA 98188-3905 USA
(206) 574-0440
www.cascadeyarns.com

Fiesta Yarns
5401 San Diego NE
Albuquerque, NM 87113-2901 USA
(505) 892-5008
www.fiestayarns.com

Fire Mountain Gems and Beads
One Fire Mountain Way
Grants Pass, OR 97526 USA
(800) 355-2137
www.firemountaingems.com

Interlacements
P.O. Box 3082
Colorado Springs, CO 80934-3082 USA
(719) 578-8009
www.interlacementsyarns.com

Kolláge Yarns
3304 Blue Bell Lane
Birmingham, AL 35242 USA
(205) 908-1570
www.kollageyarns.com

Kraemer Yarns
P.O. Box 72
240 S. Main Street
Nazareth, PA 18064-0072 USA
(610) 759-4030
www.kraemeryarns.com

Lorna's Laces
(773) 935-3803
www.lornaslaces.net

157

Louet North America
808 Commerce Park Drive
Ogdensburg, NY 13669 USA
(613) 925-4502
www.louet.com

Mountain Colors
P.O. Box 156
Corvallis, MT 59828 USA
(406) 961-1900
www.mountaincolors.com

Muench Yarns Inc.
1323 Scott Street
Petaluma, CA 94954 USA
(707) 763-9377
www.muenchyarns.com
www.myyarns.com

Plymouth Yarn Co., Inc.
P.O. Box 28
Bristol, PA 19007 USA
(215) 788-0459
www.plymouthyarn.com

Sewing Expressions LLC
1497 Main Street, Suite 315
Dunedin, FL 34698 USA
(727) 734-1123
www.sewingexpressions.com

South West Trading Company
918 South Park Lane, Suite 102
Tempe, AZ 85281 USA
(480) 894-1818
For a listing of local yarn stores that
carry SWTC yarns, visit
www.soysilk.com

Swarovski North America Limited
One Kenney Drive
Cranston, RI 02920 USA
(401) 447-7314
www.swarovski.com
www.create-your-style.com

Tahki Stacy Charles, Inc.
70-30 80th Street, Bldg. 36
Ridgewood, NY 11385 USA
(800) 338-YARN
www.tahkistacycharles.com

Tilli Tomas, Inc.
Boston, MA USA
(617) 524-3330
www.tillitomas.com

About the Authors

Anastasia Blaes and Kelly Wilson are revitalizing knitting and crochet technique with their focus on innovative constructions. Not afraid to push the envelope, they apply traditional techniques in a nontraditional manner to create garments and accessories that ignite the passions of knitters and crocheters, beginner and experienced alike. Anastasia owns Anastasiaknits, home of Yarn Cocktails *purse-size patterns; Kelly owns Kelly Wilson Designs.*

Acknowledgments

Many thanks to Mary Ann Hall, for taking us under your wing and helping us make a dream possible. Thank you, Rochelle Bourgault, for your excellent project management. Many thanks to Regina Grenier for your fantastic art direction. We appreciate everyone at Rockport for embracing the concept of this book, and for your creativity. Big thanks to Jean Lampe, for your excellent technical editing. It's been a pleasure working with you. Thank you to Judy Love for bringing the techniques to life with your illustrations.

Thanks a million to our families. Our husbands pitched in and helped tremendously, as did our parents. We are very thankful for everyone's patience and understanding while we concentrated on our designing. Special thanks to our children whose laughter and kisses helped us meet deadlines.

We appreciate all of the companies listed in the resource section who provided superb products for the designs. Here's to luscious yarns, sparkling beads, and fabulous people.

Thank you, Claire Wudowsky, for always having a shoulder to lean on.

And here's to you, crocheters. Thank you for purchasing this book. We hope you will have a delicious experience with our *Yarn Cocktails* designs.